ABODE

by haley roisum

ISBN: 9798862736045

This book is dedicated to

my husband, Chris, who I'm absolutely crazy about;

my parents, who are forever my biggest cheerleaders;

and

those that continue to support me in my varying adventures.

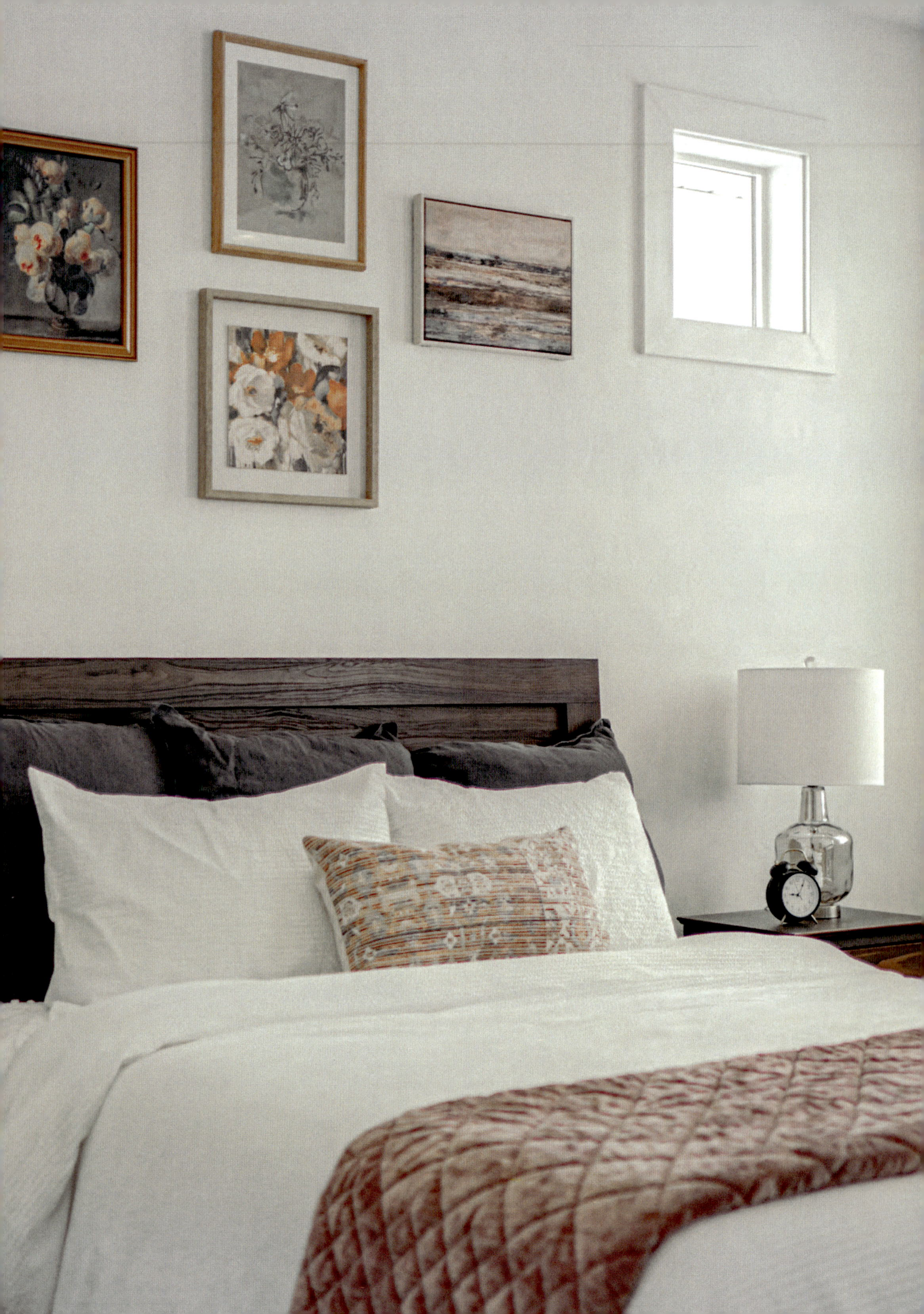

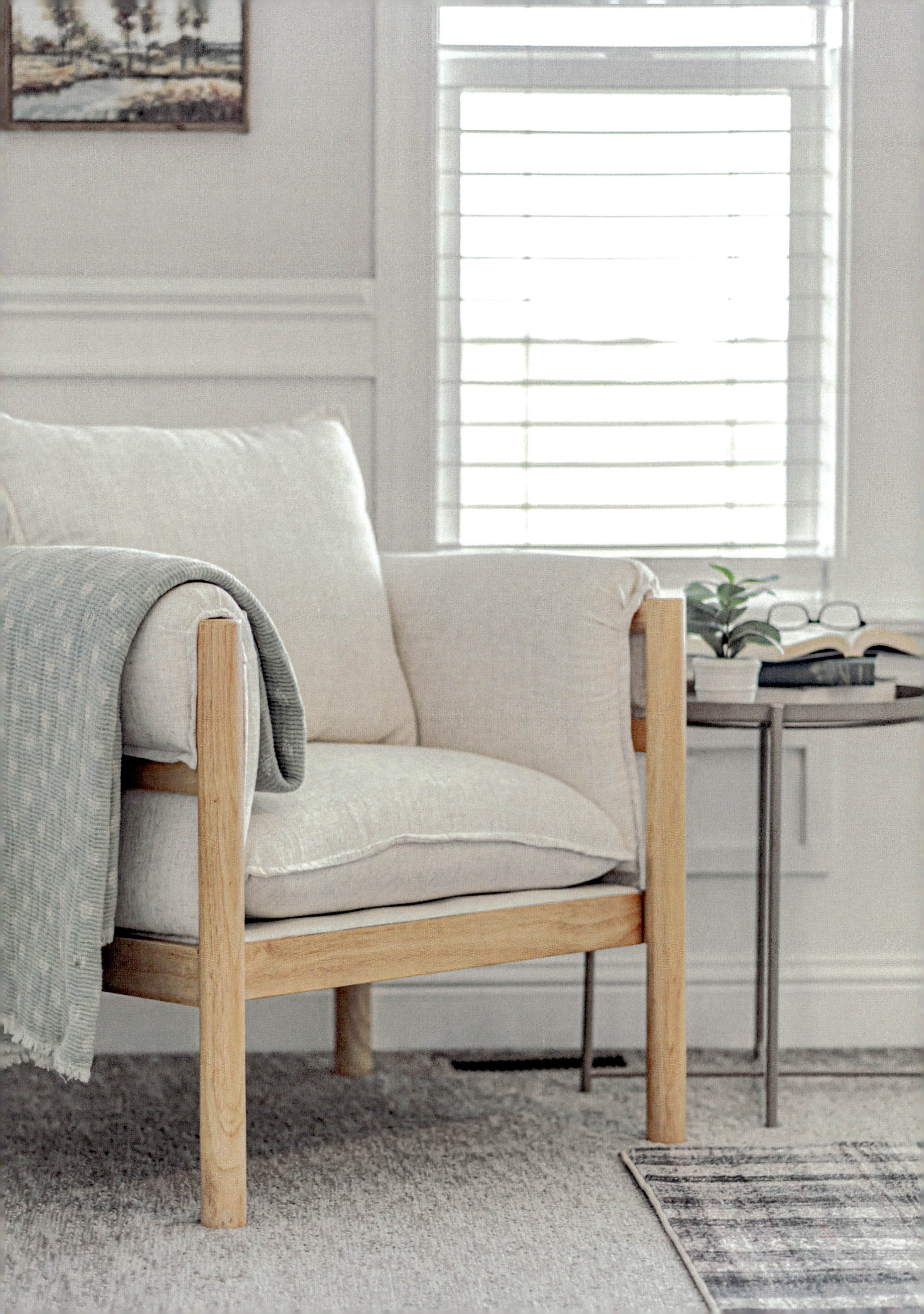

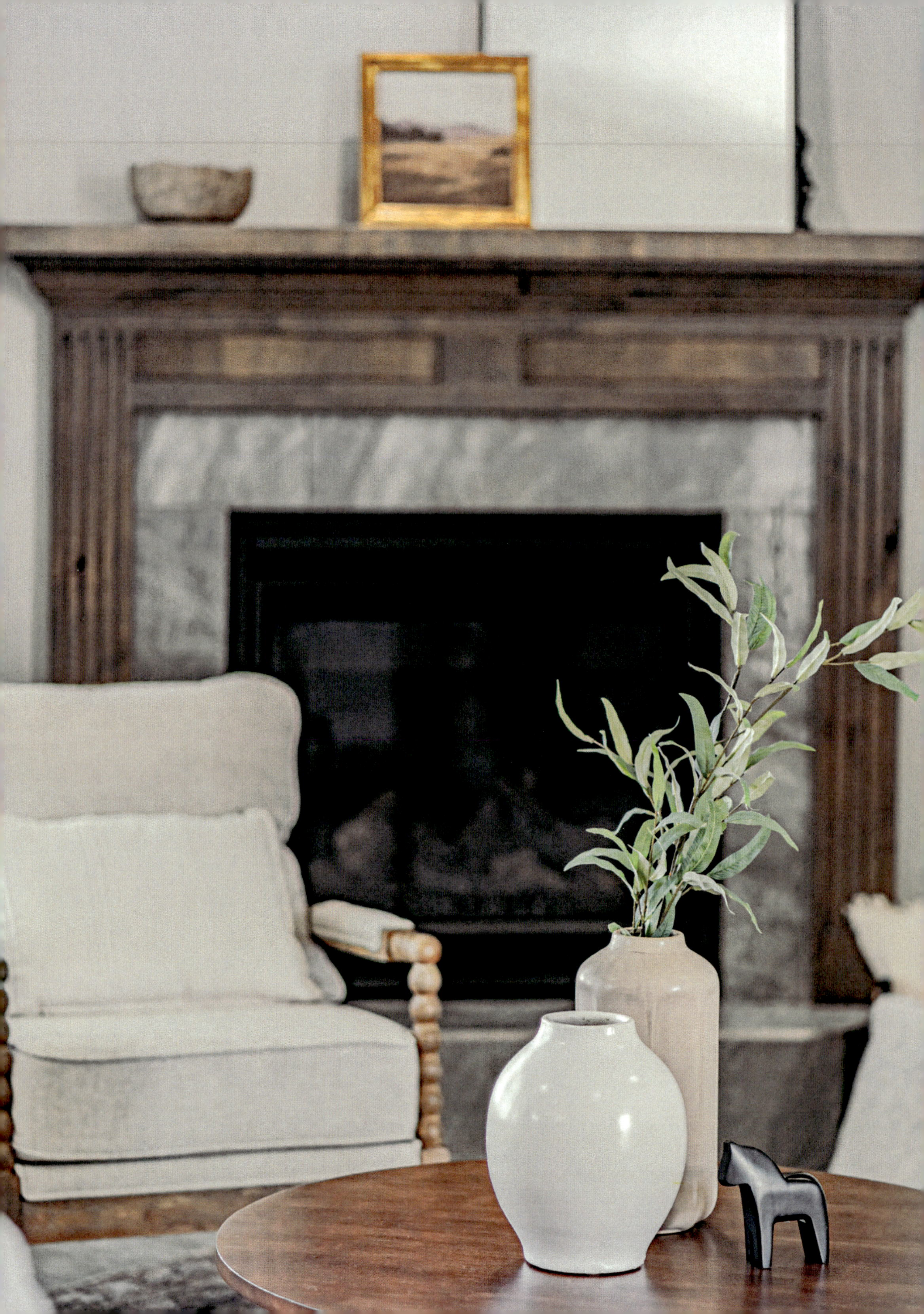

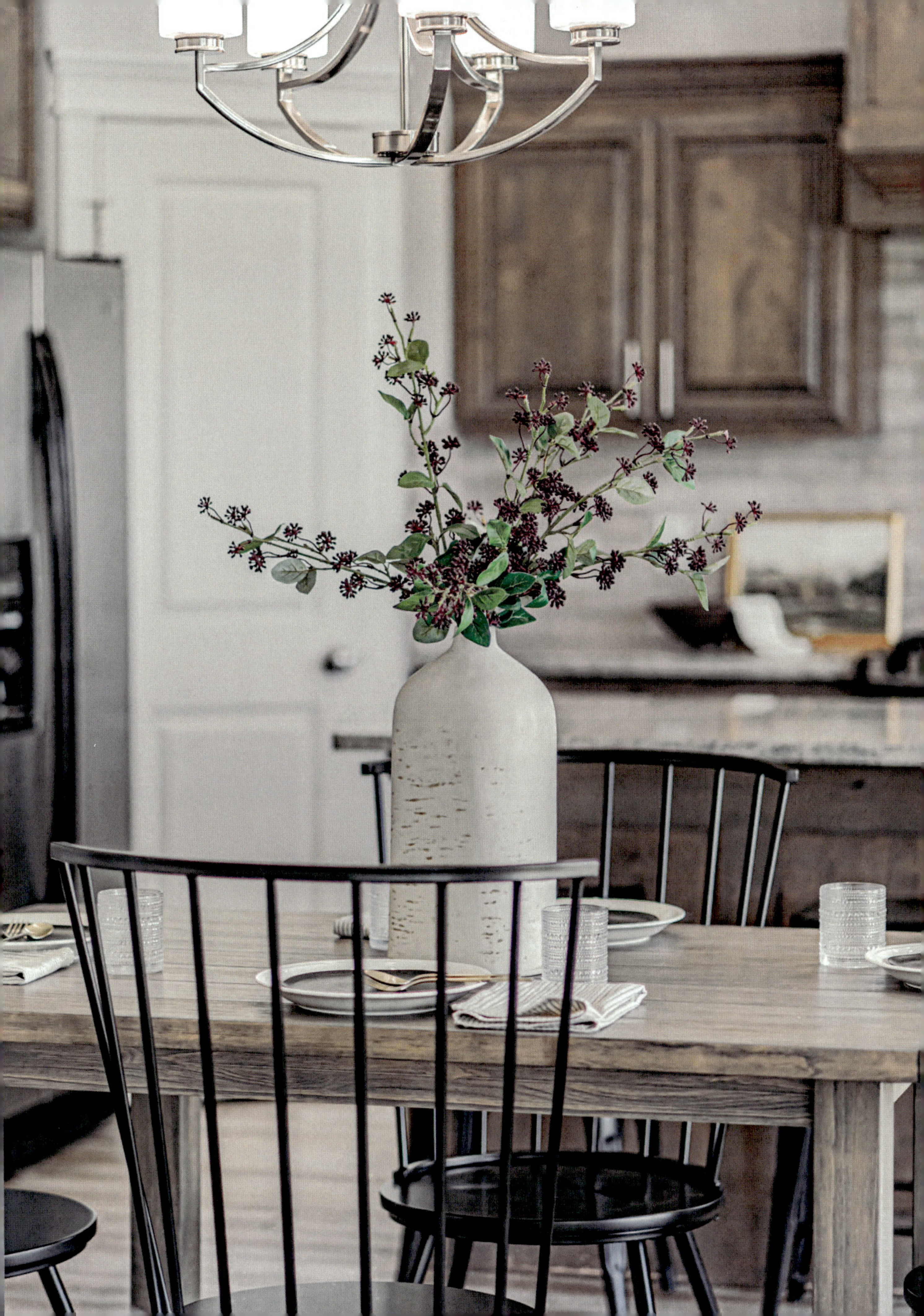

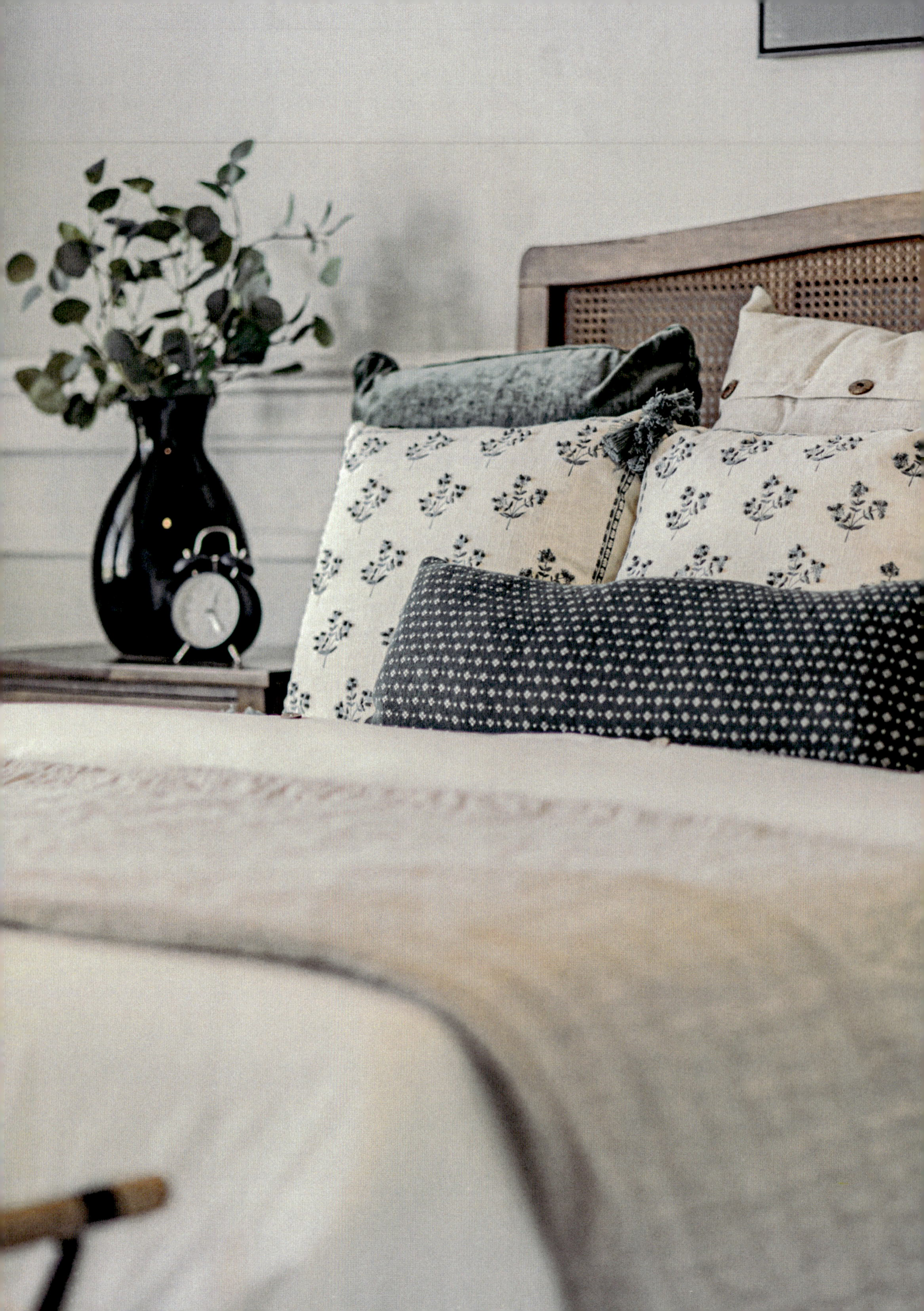

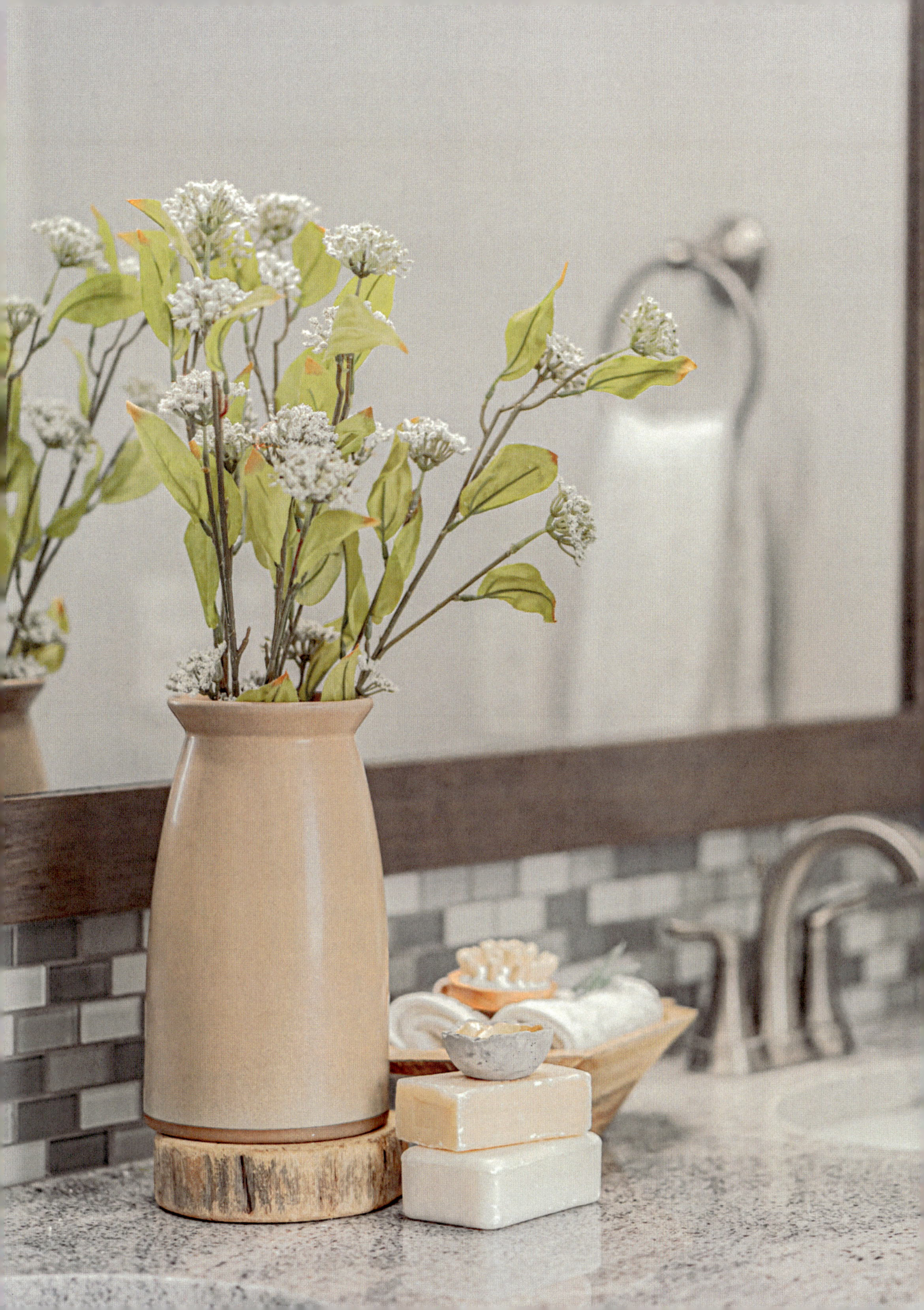

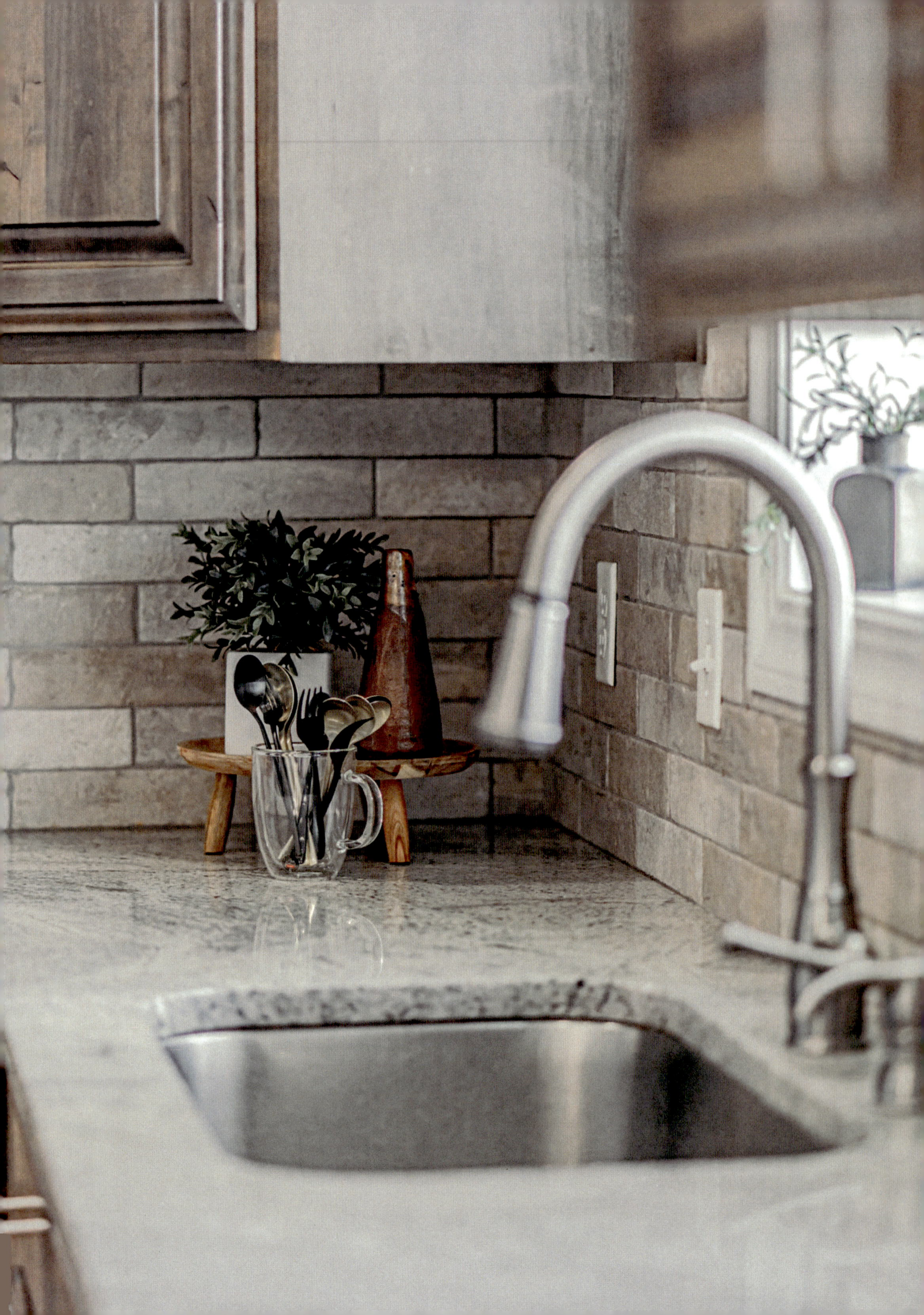

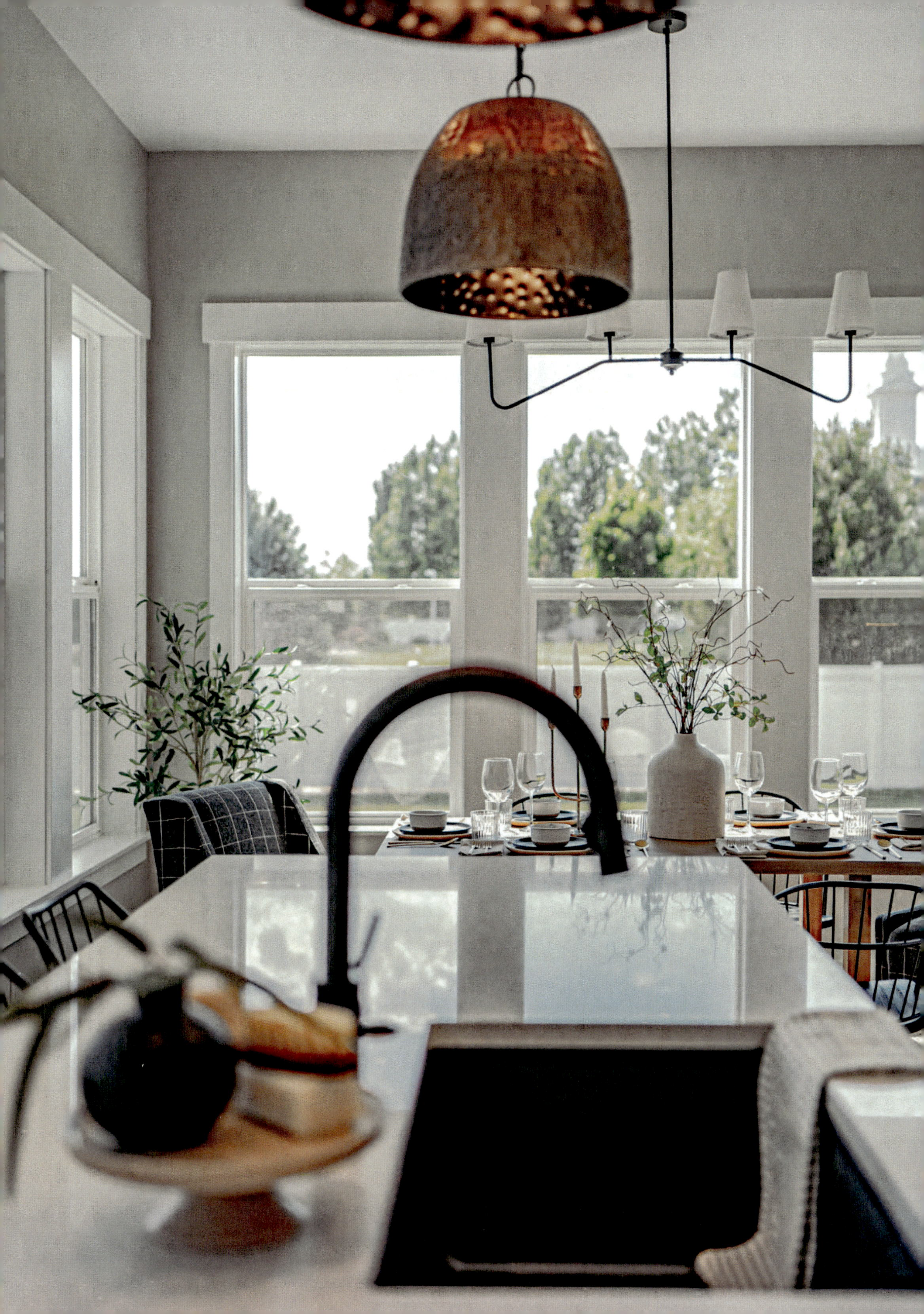

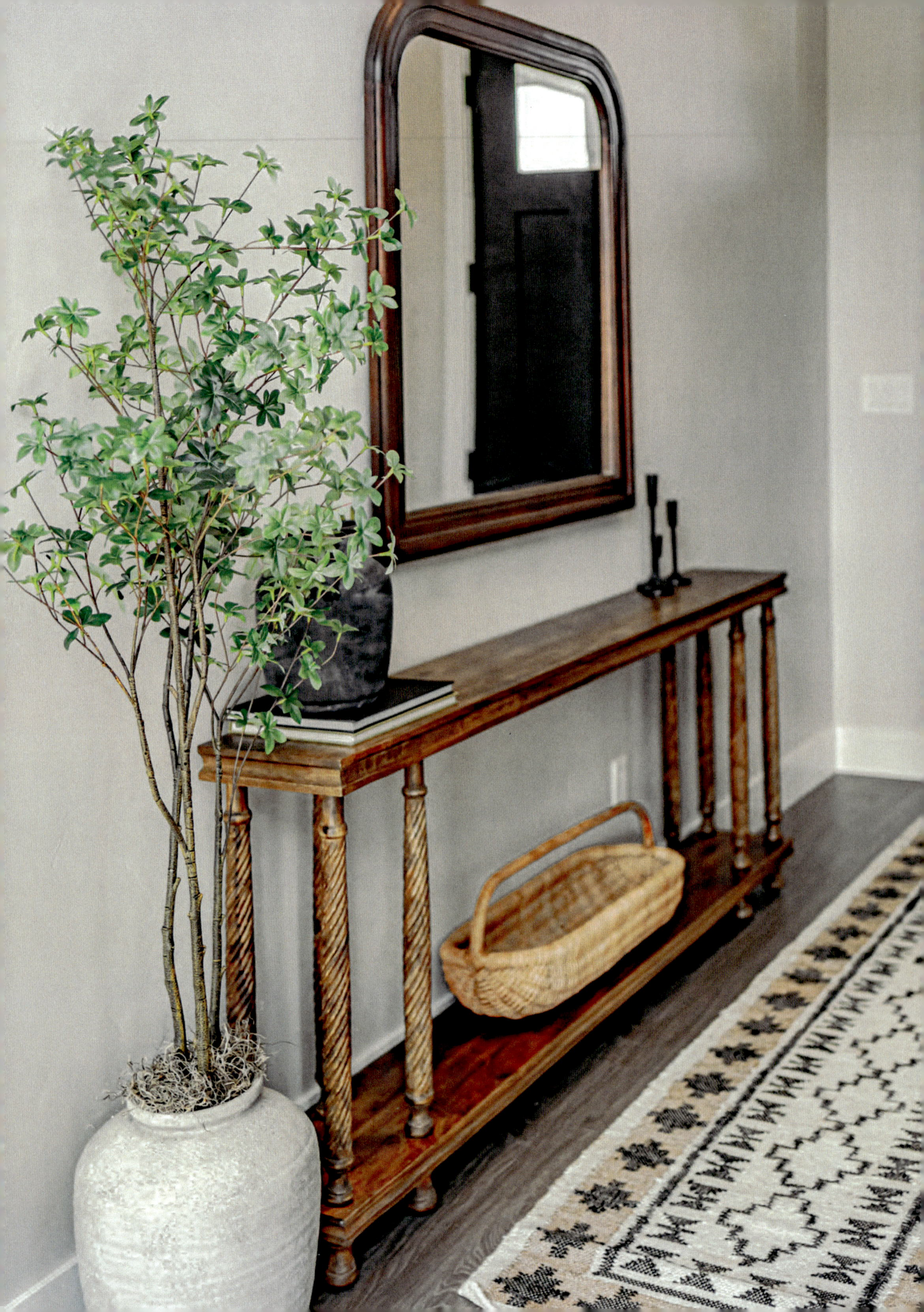

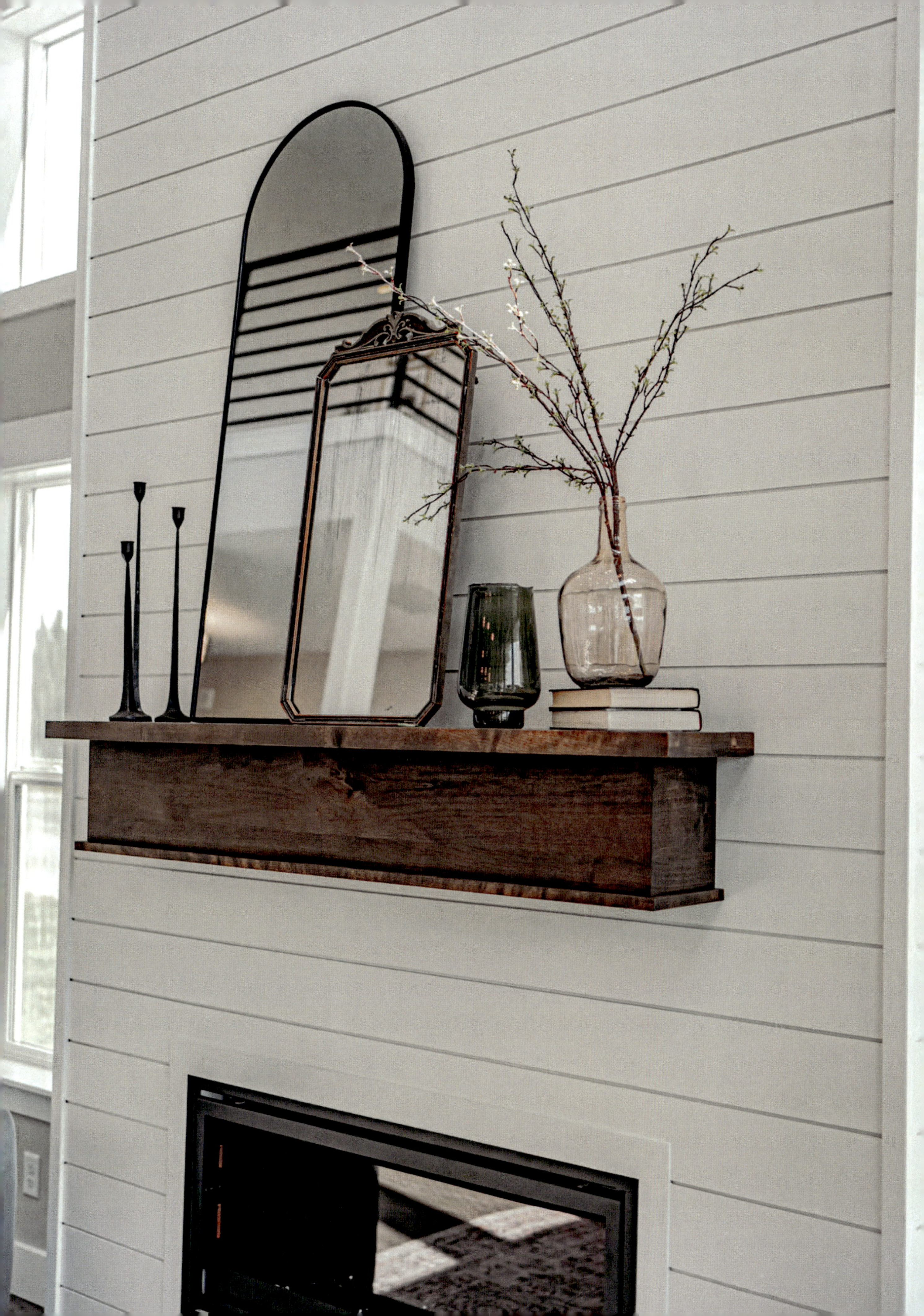

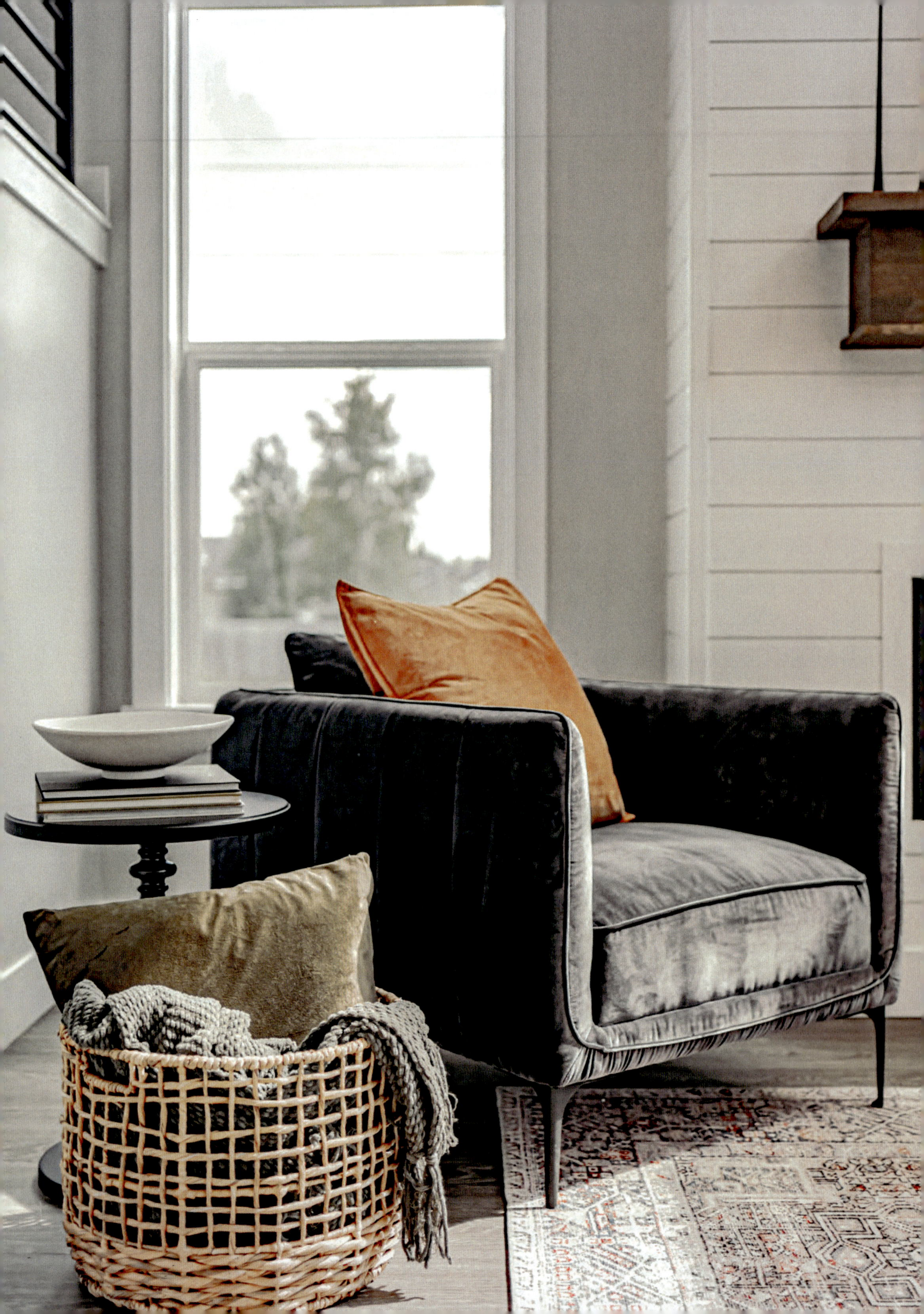

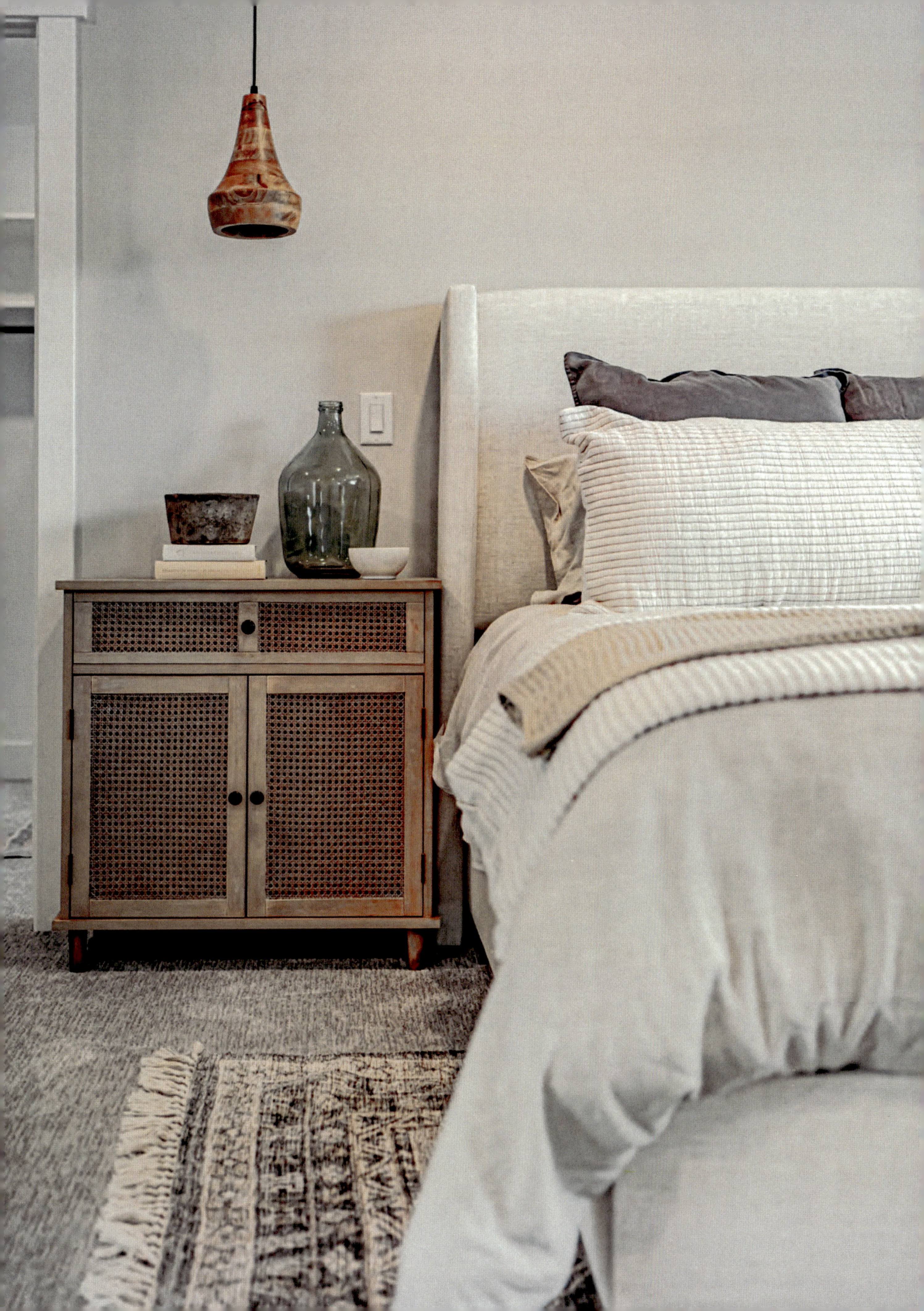

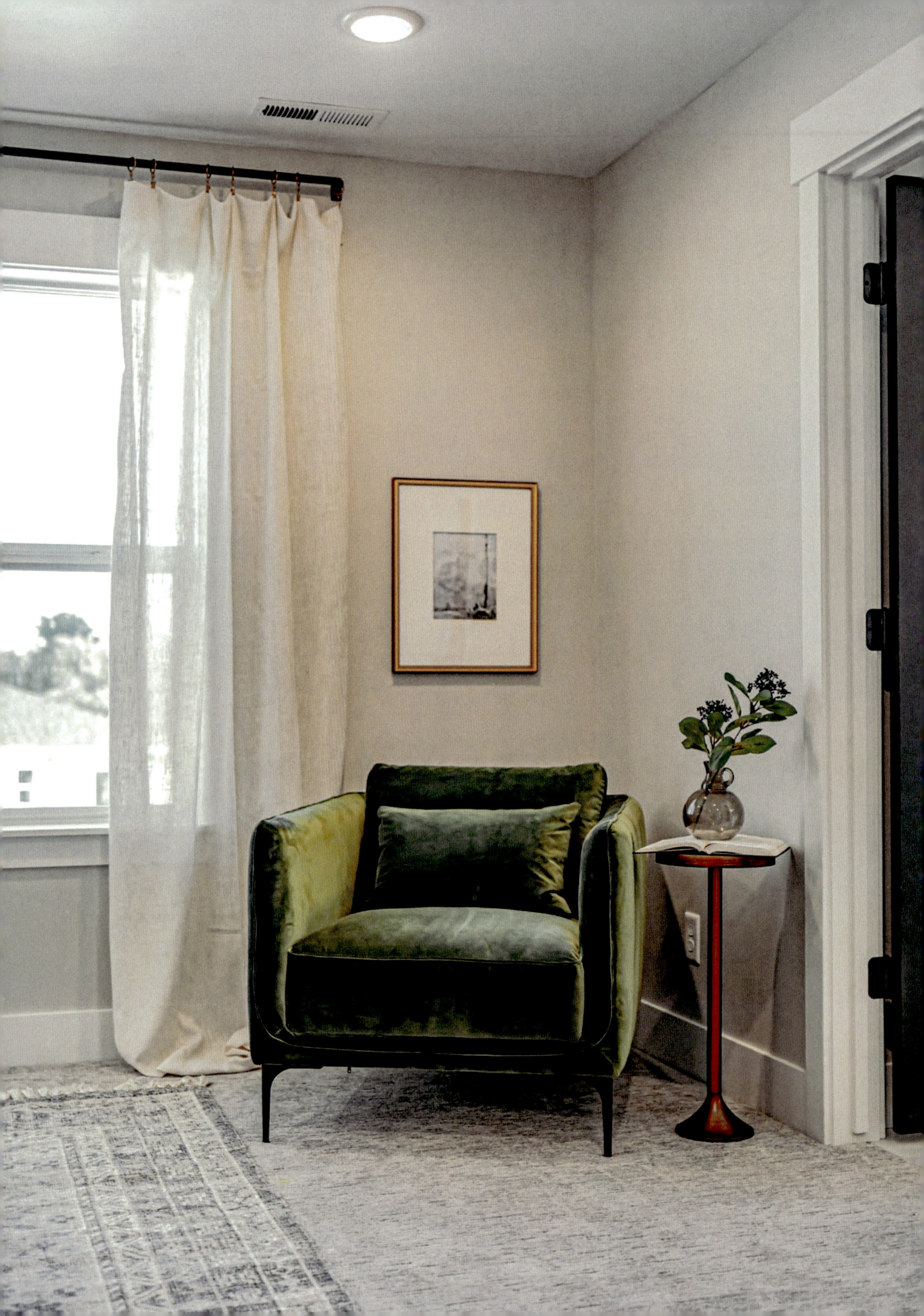

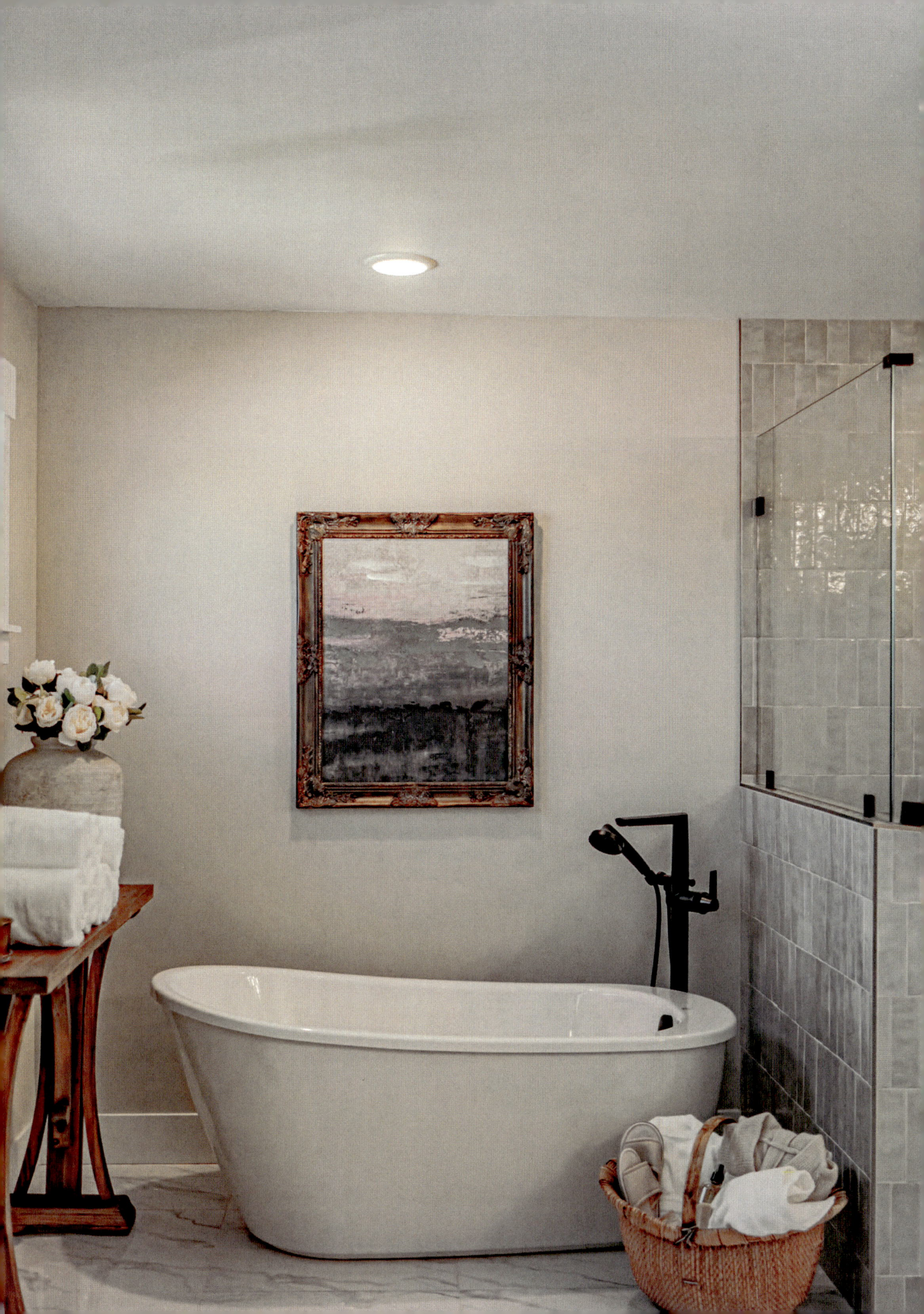

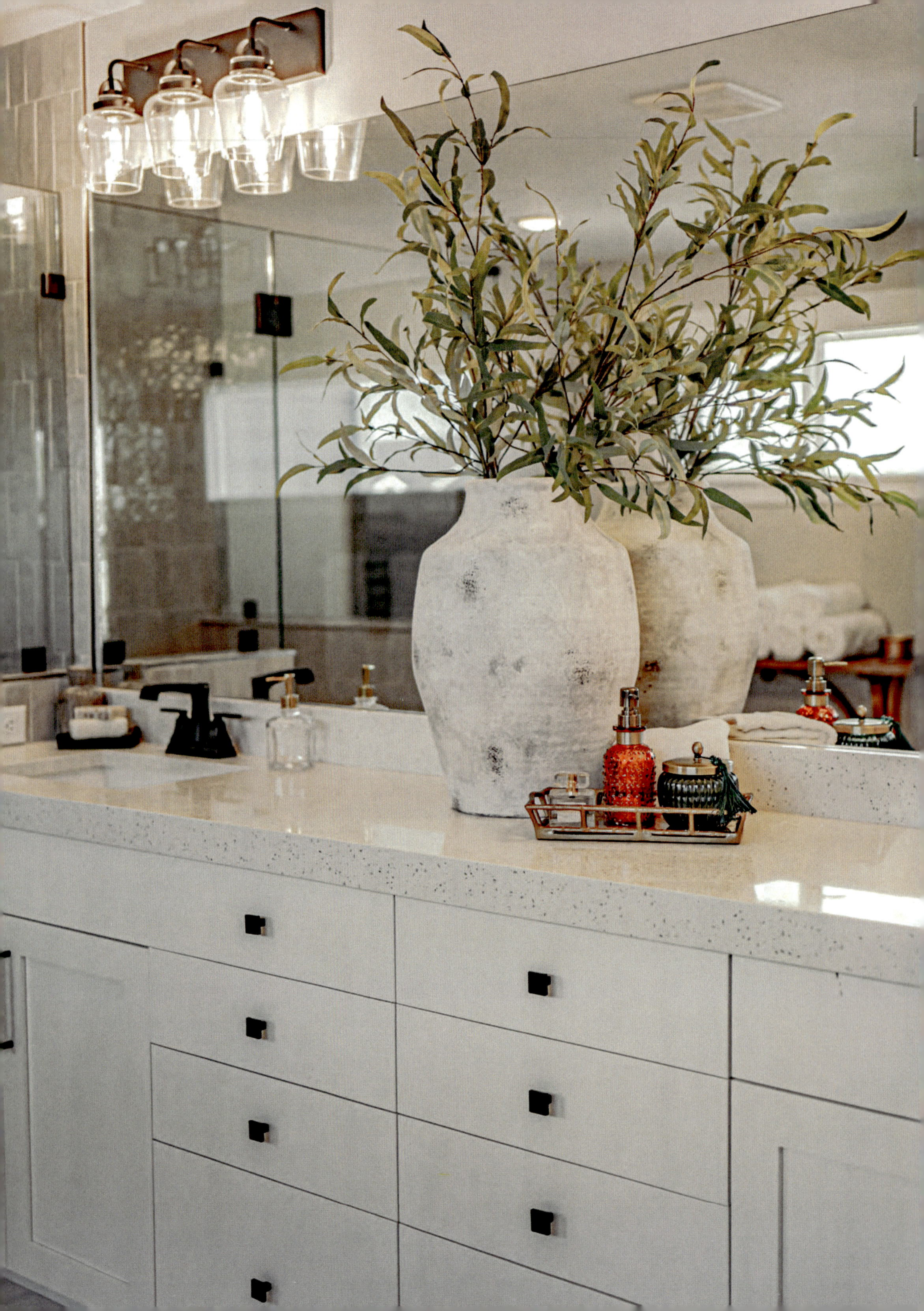

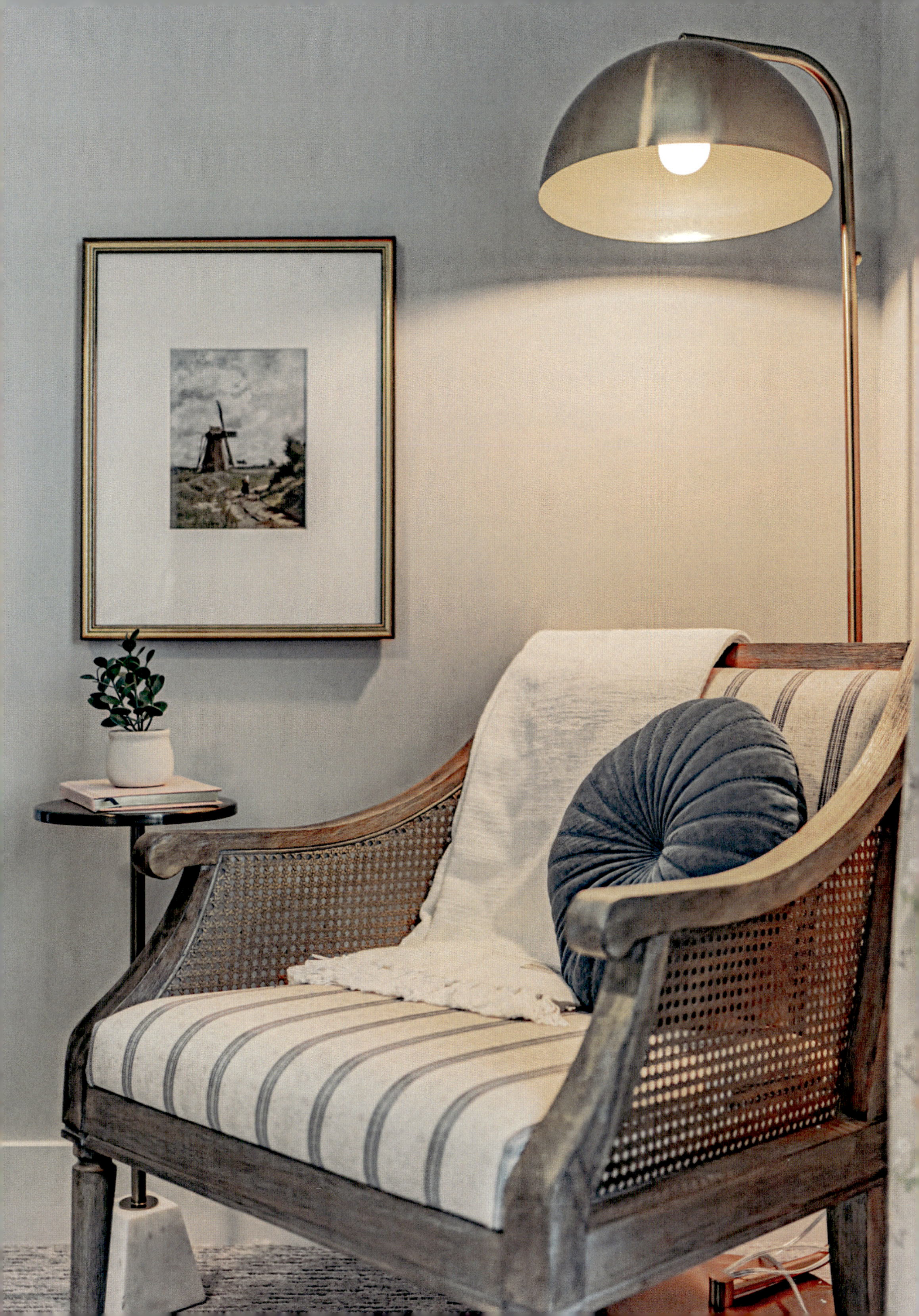

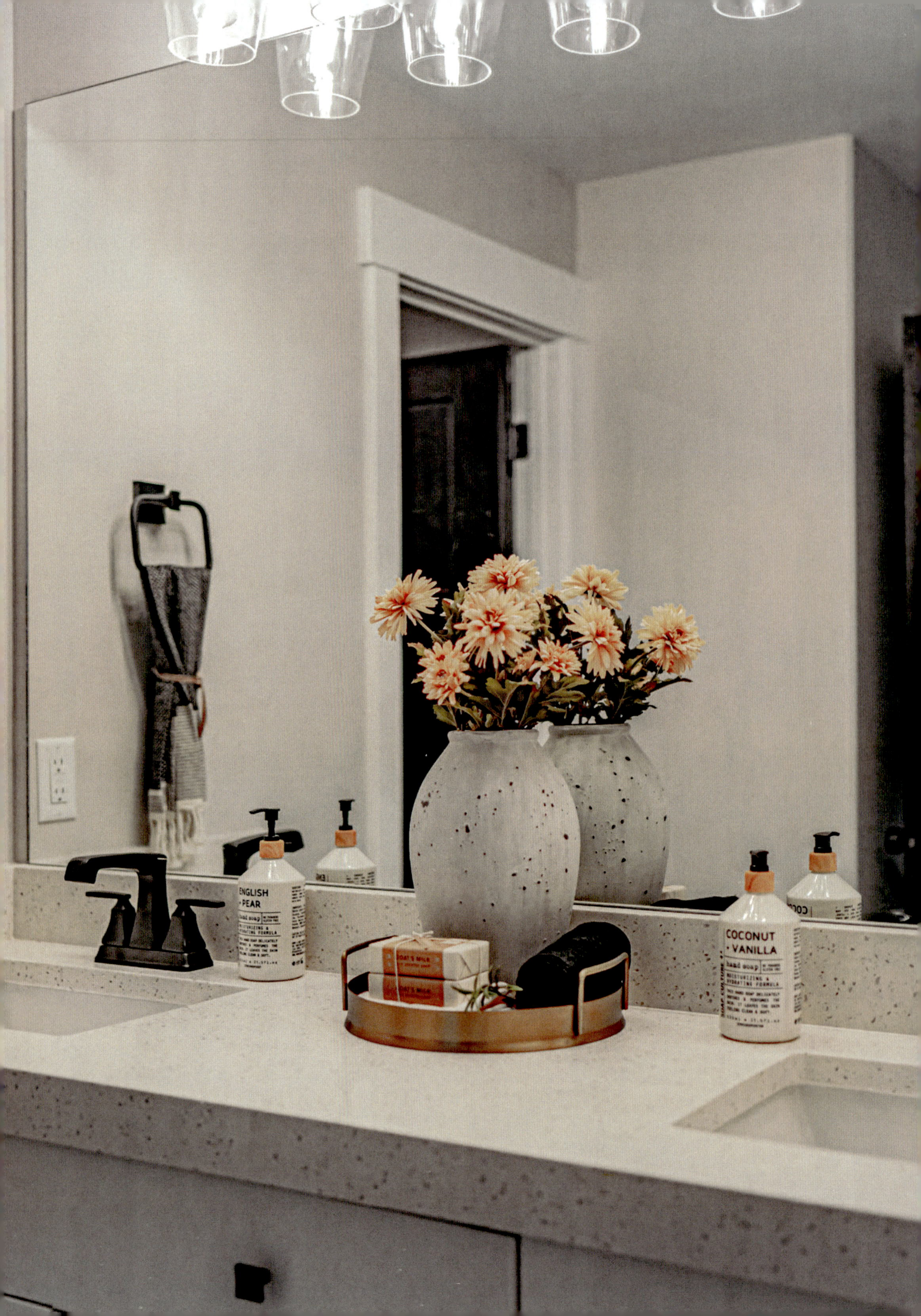
ENGLISH
+ PEAR
COCONUT
+ VANILLA
hand soap

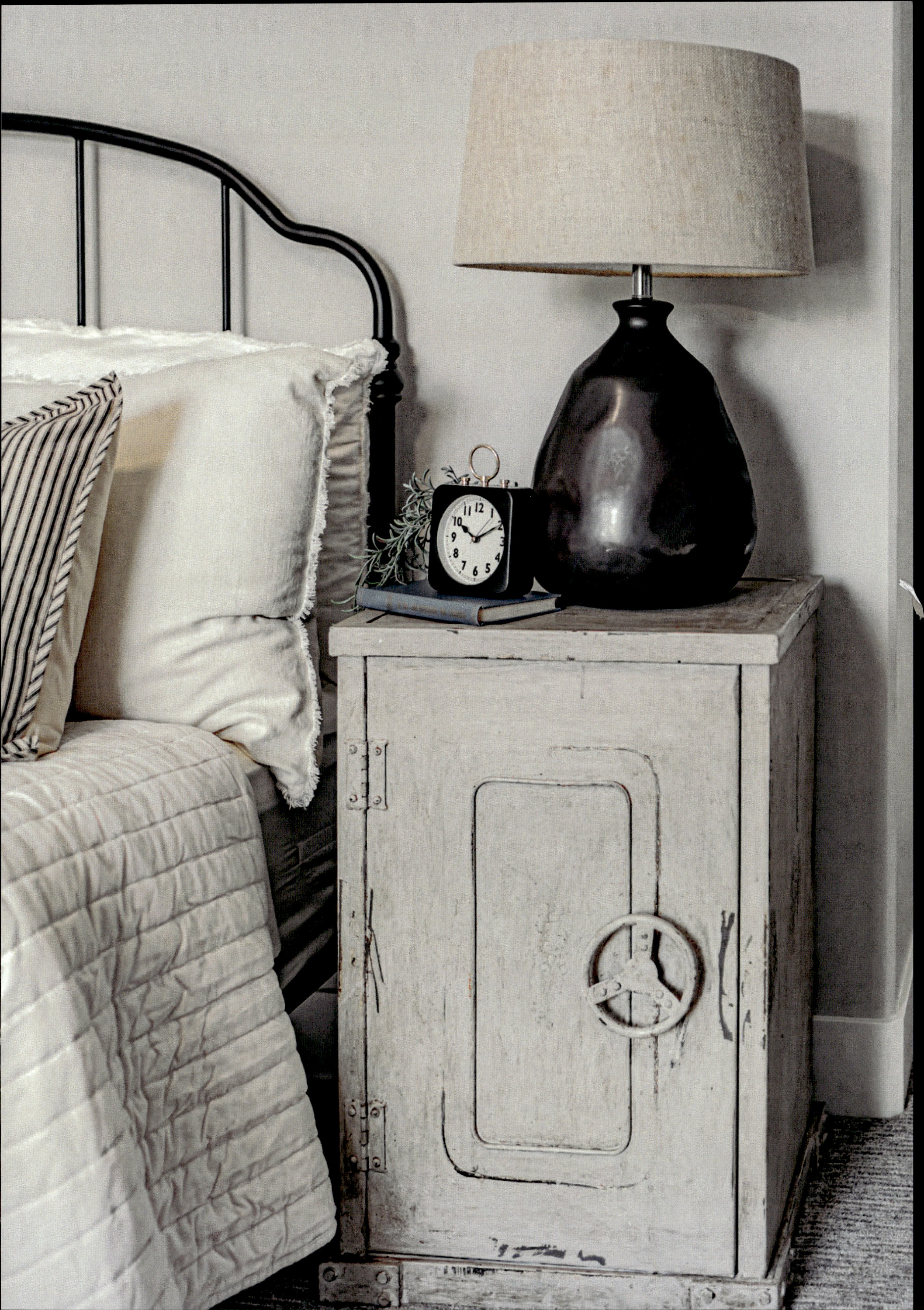

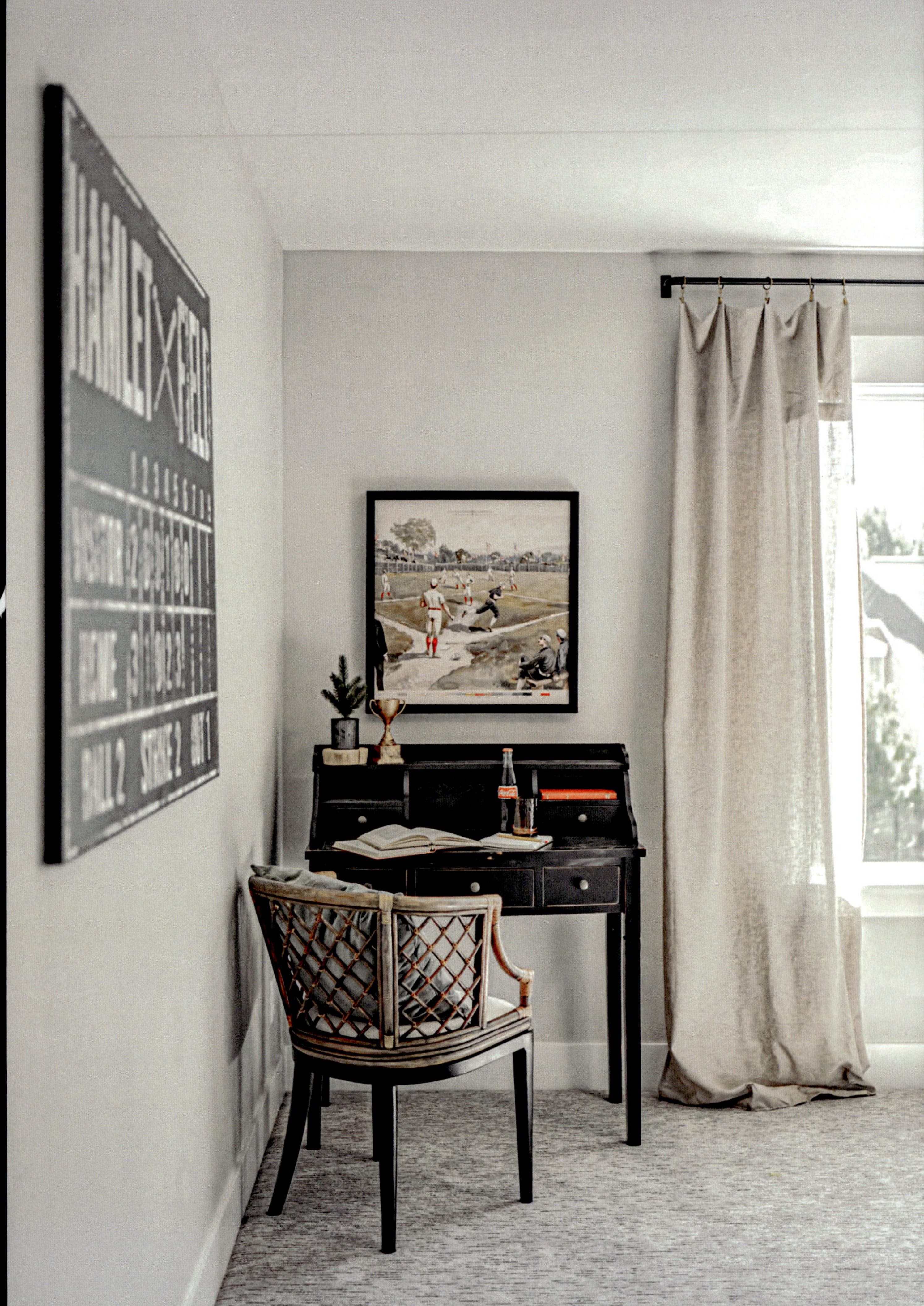
HAMLET
VISITOR
HOME
BALL 2
STRIKE 2
OUT 1

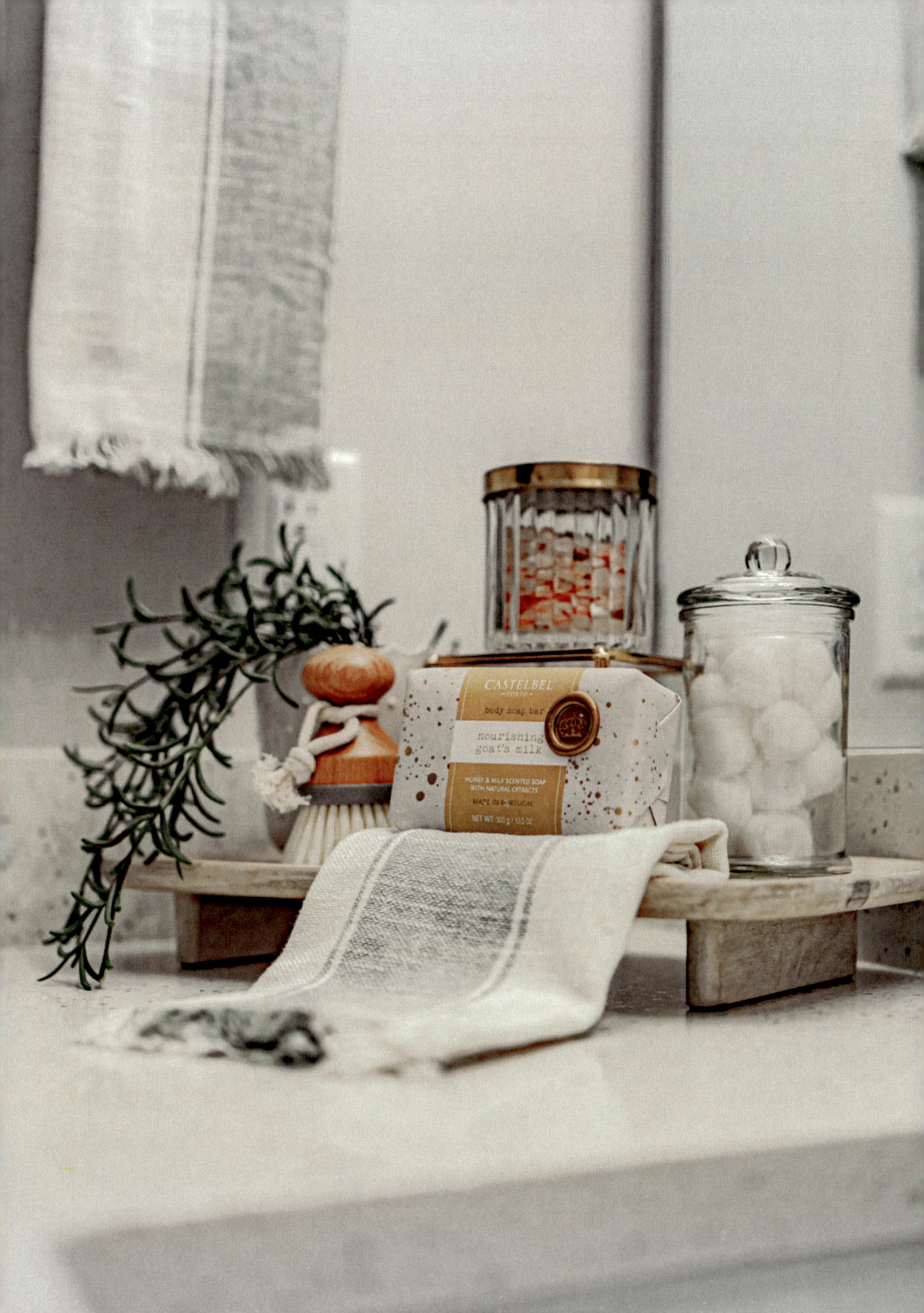
CASTELBEL
PORTO
body soap bar
nourishing
goat's milk
HONEY & MILK SCENTED SOAP
WITH NATURAL EXTRACTS

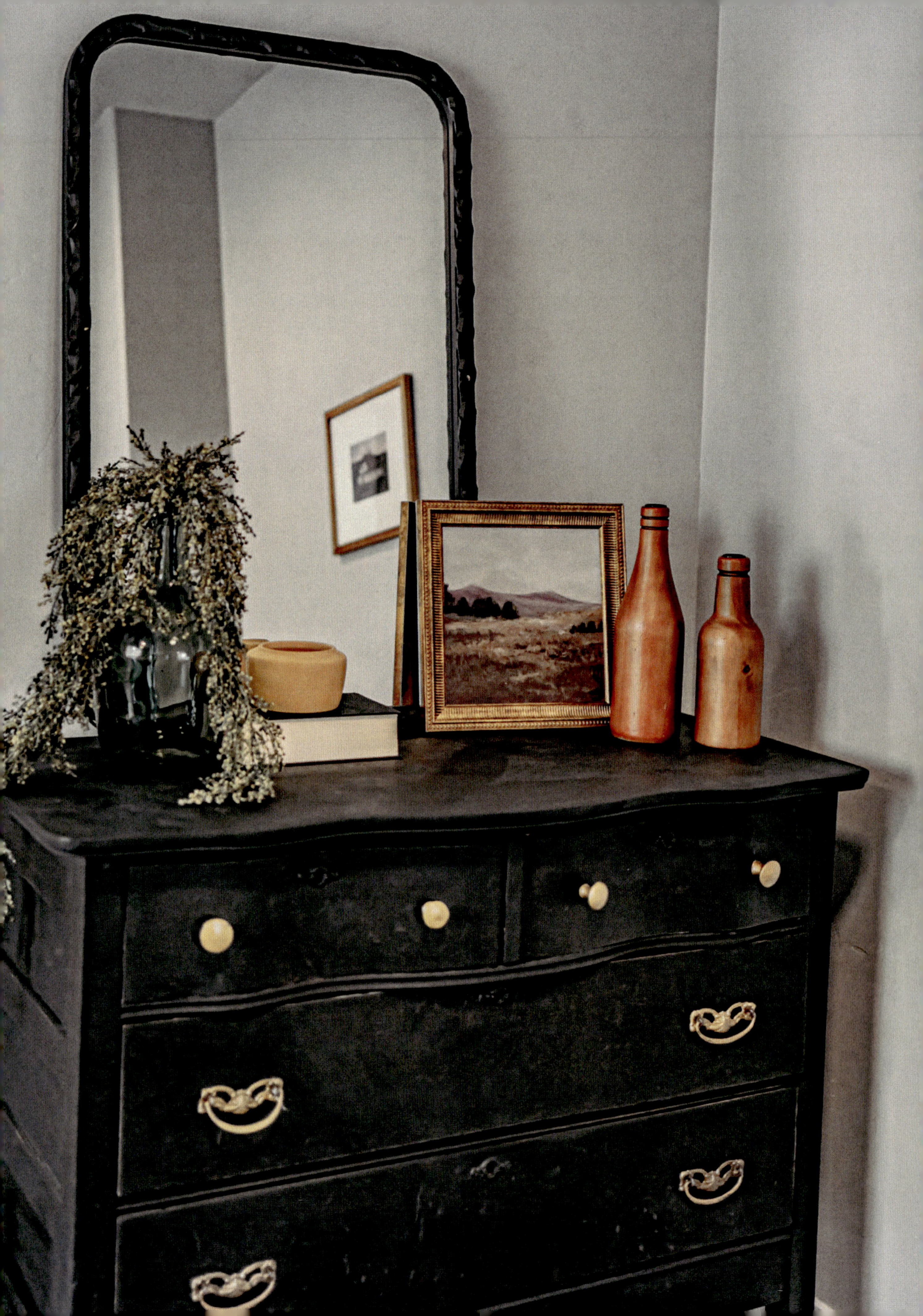

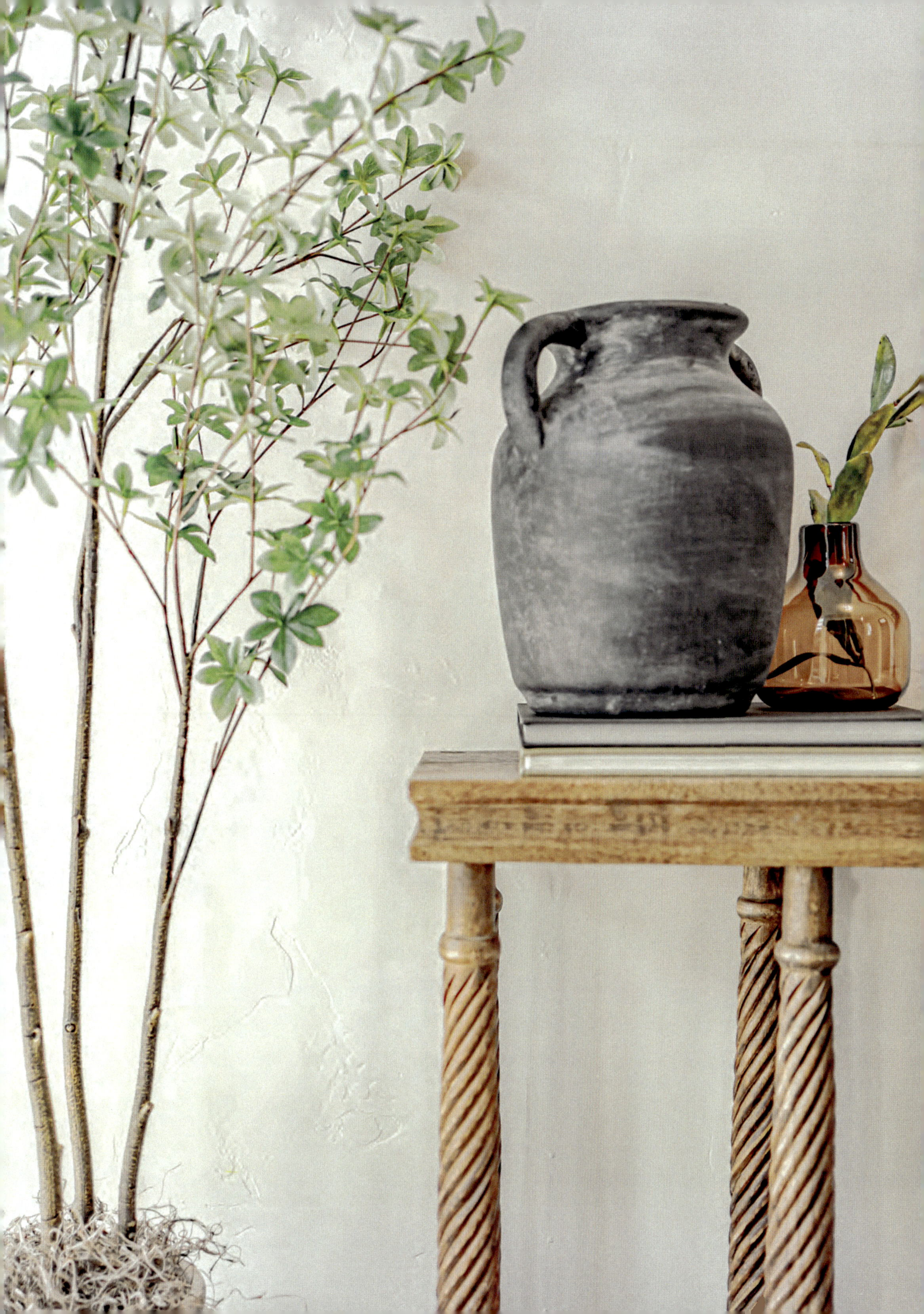

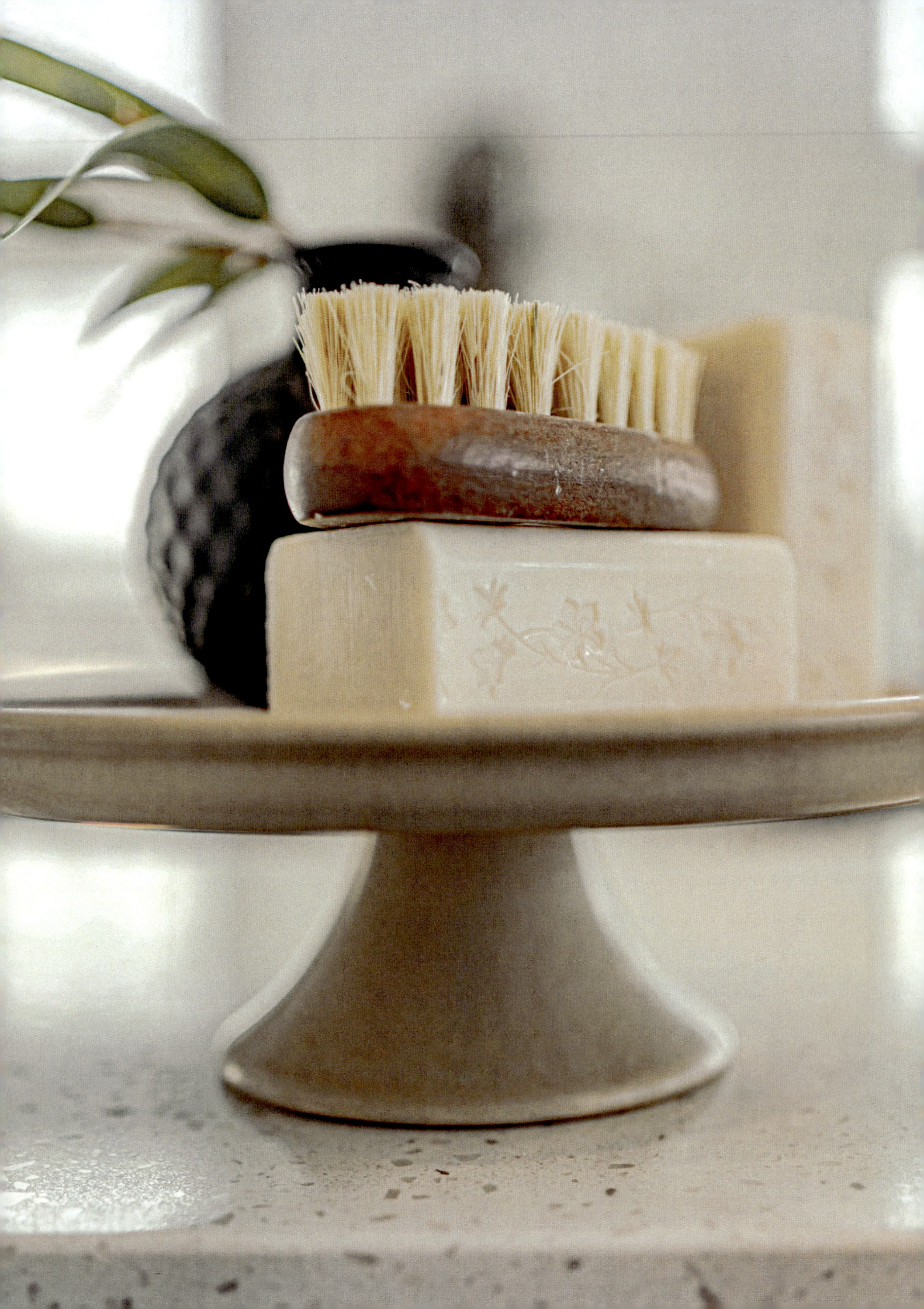

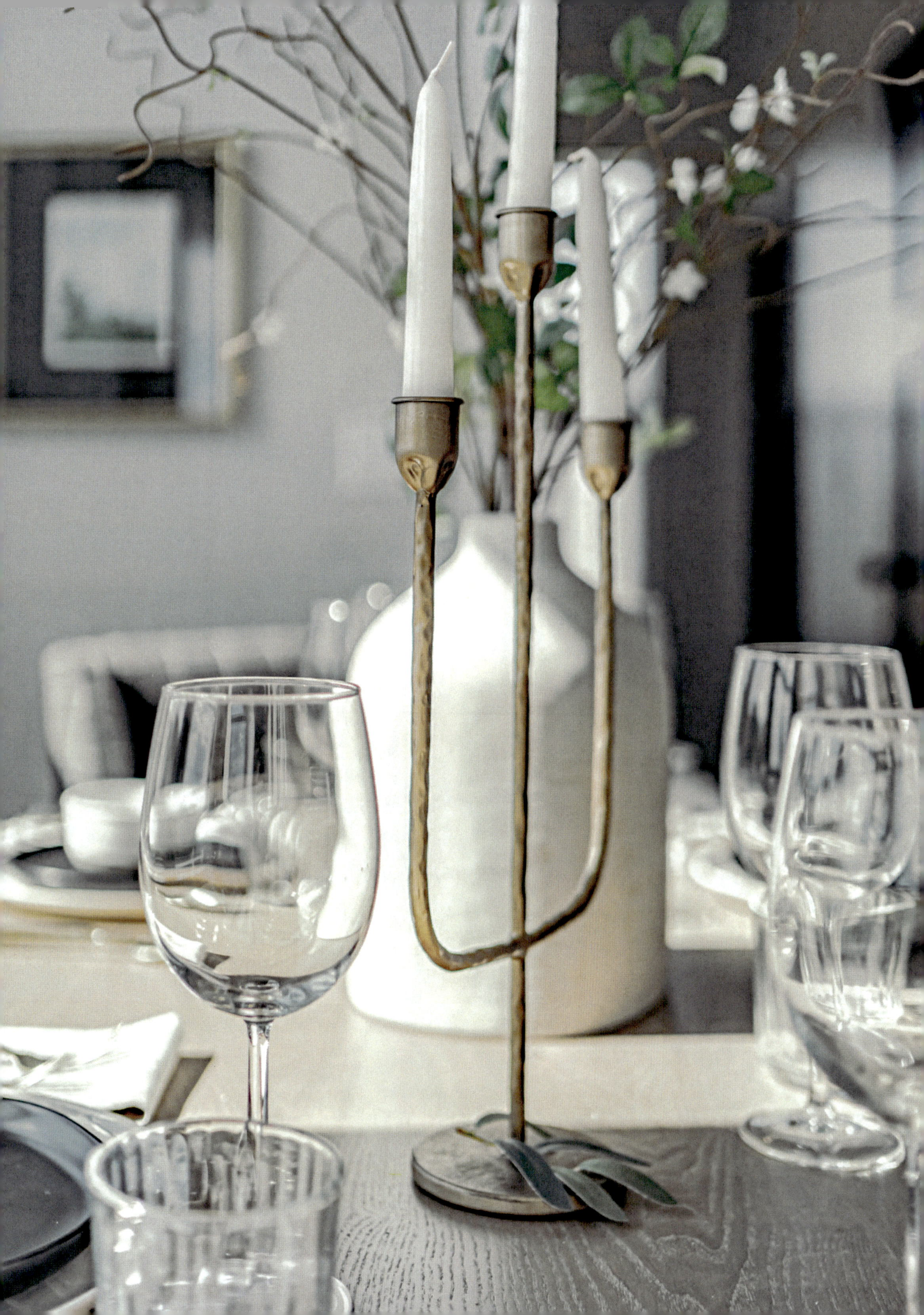

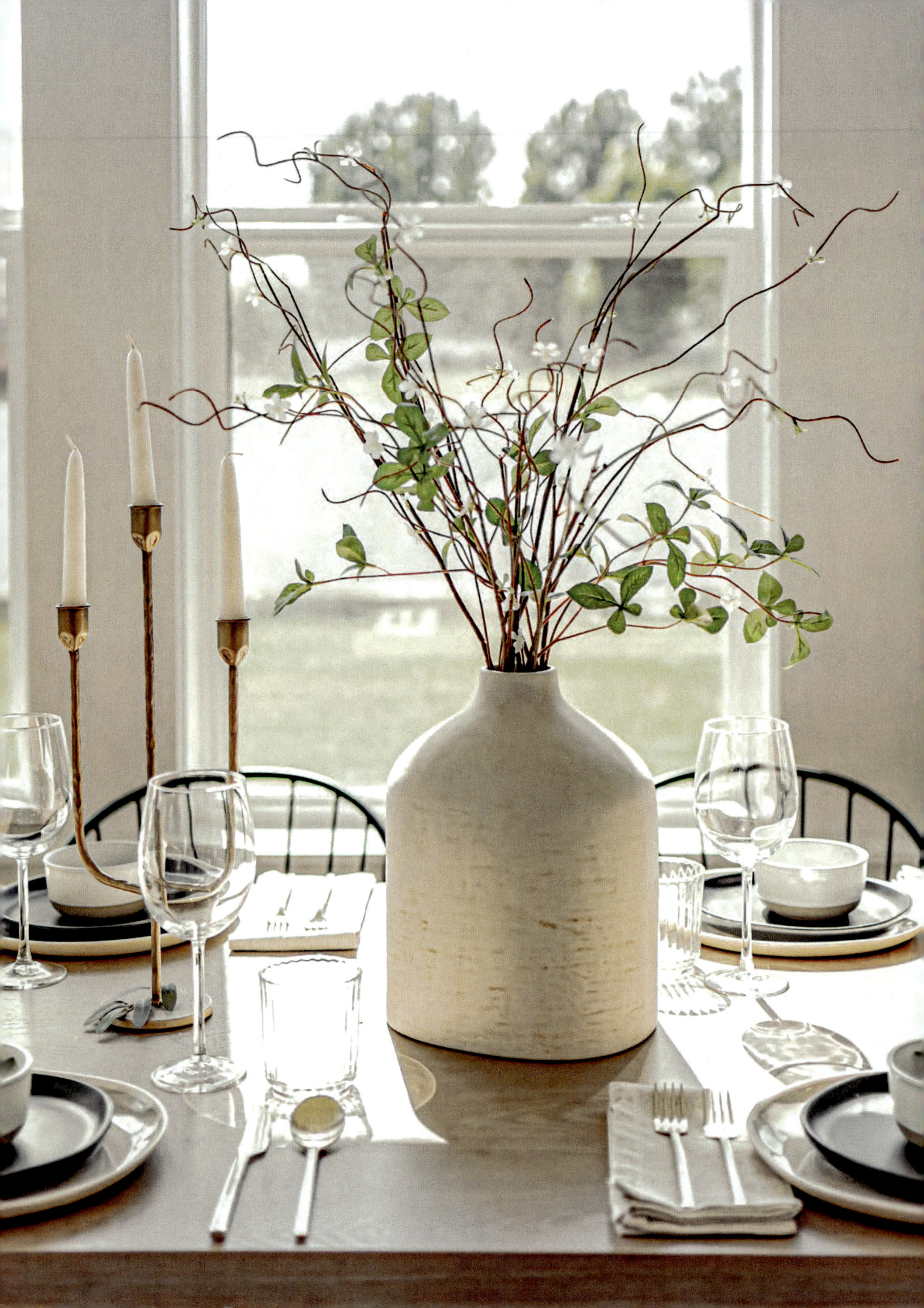

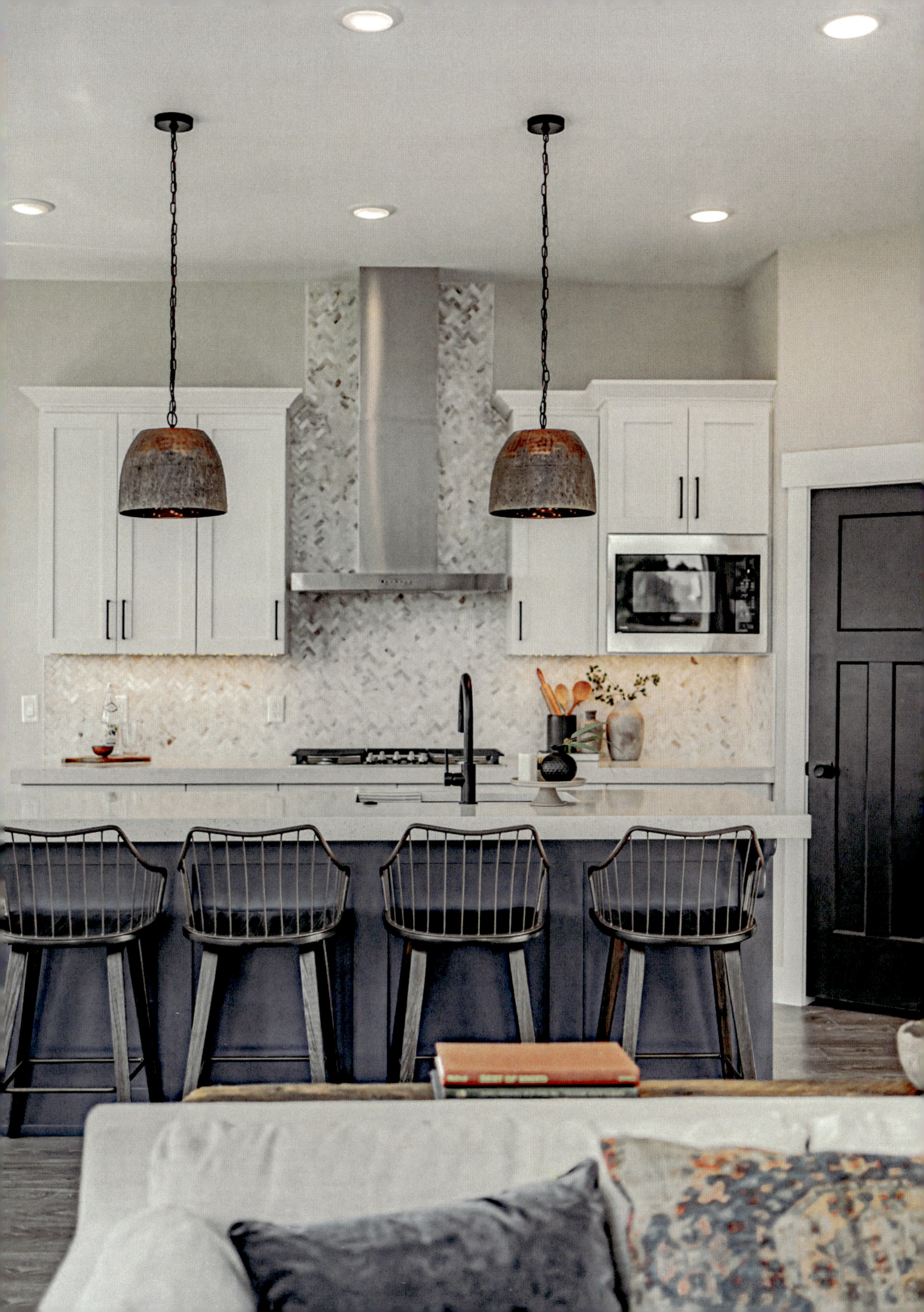

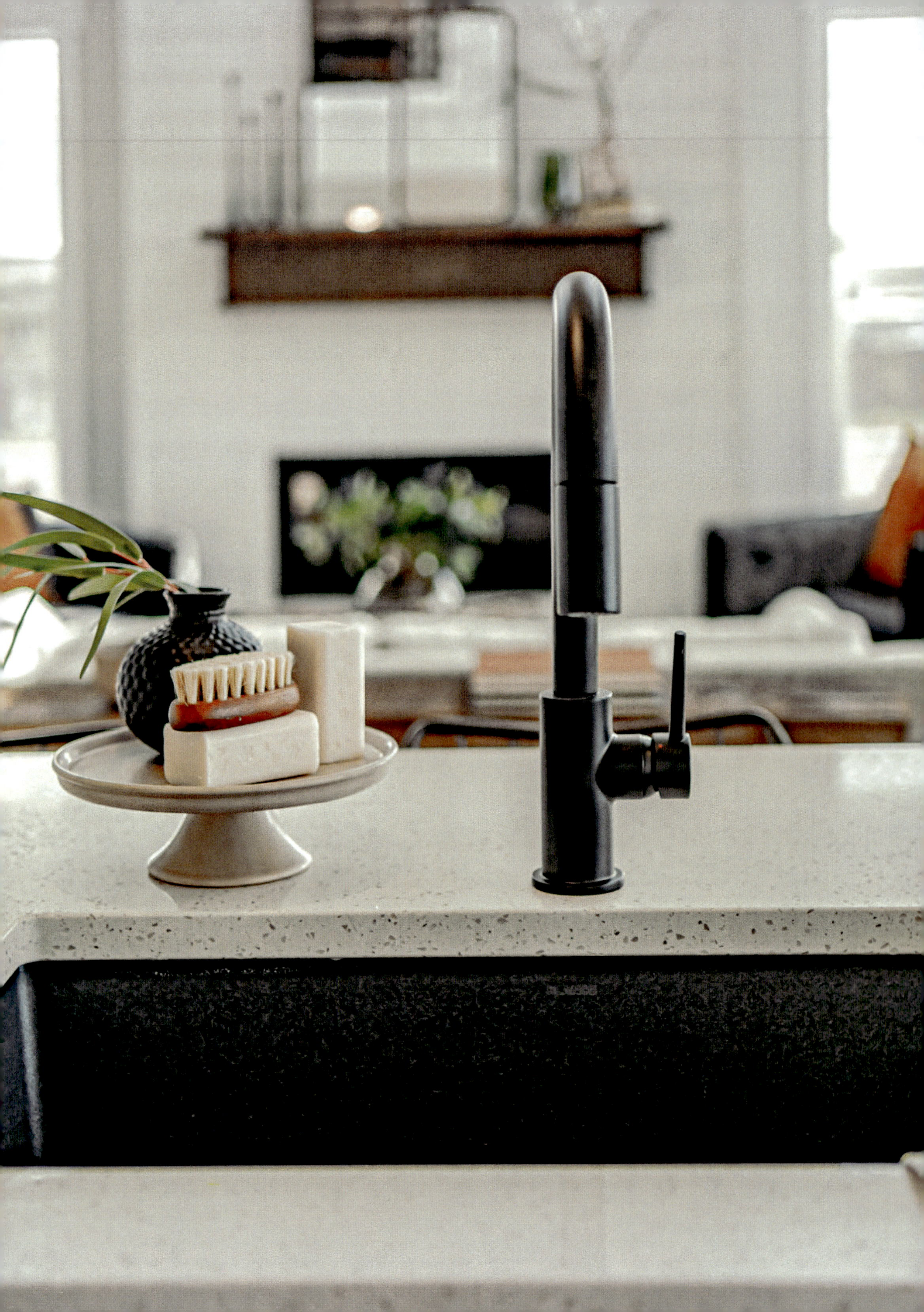

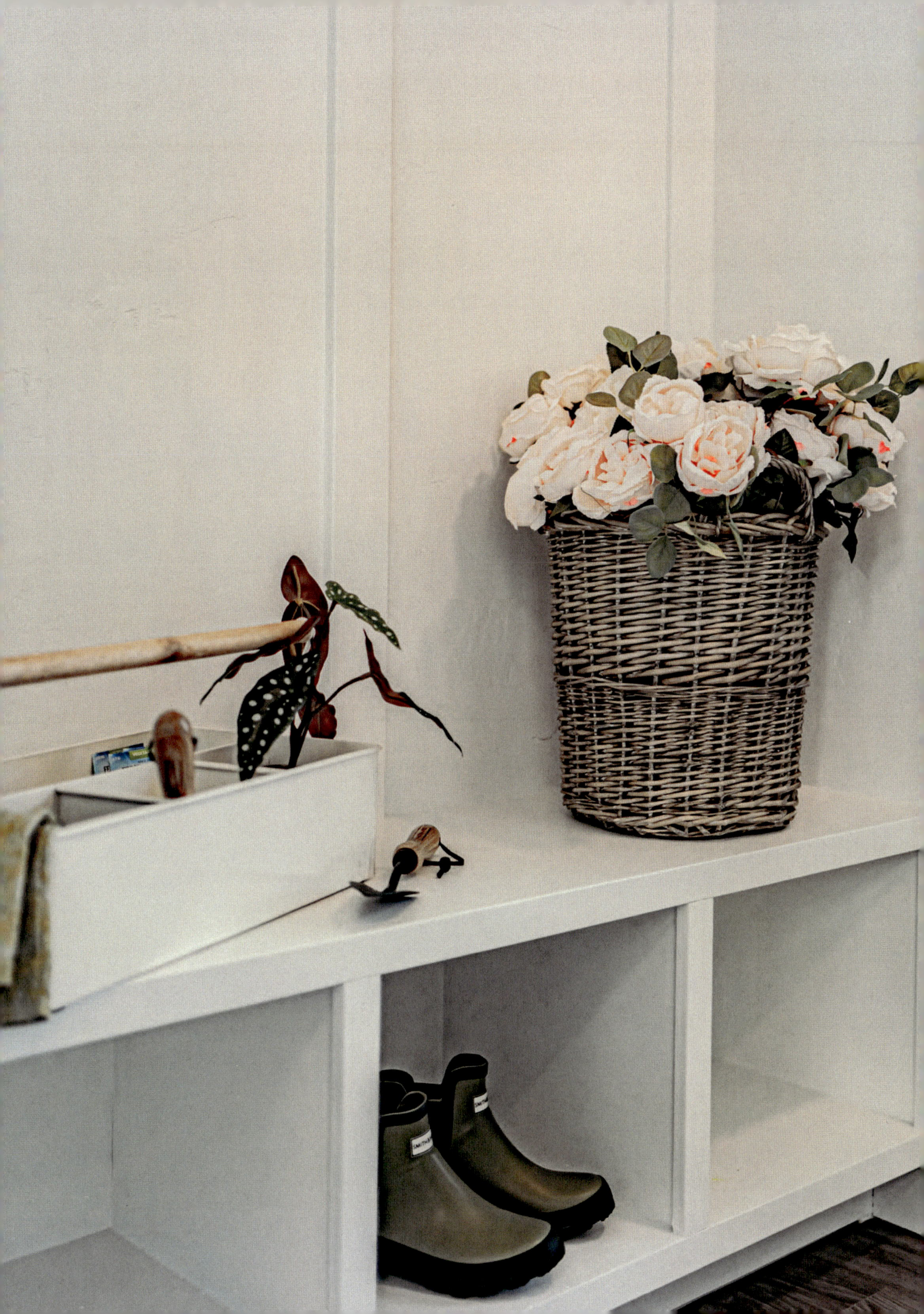

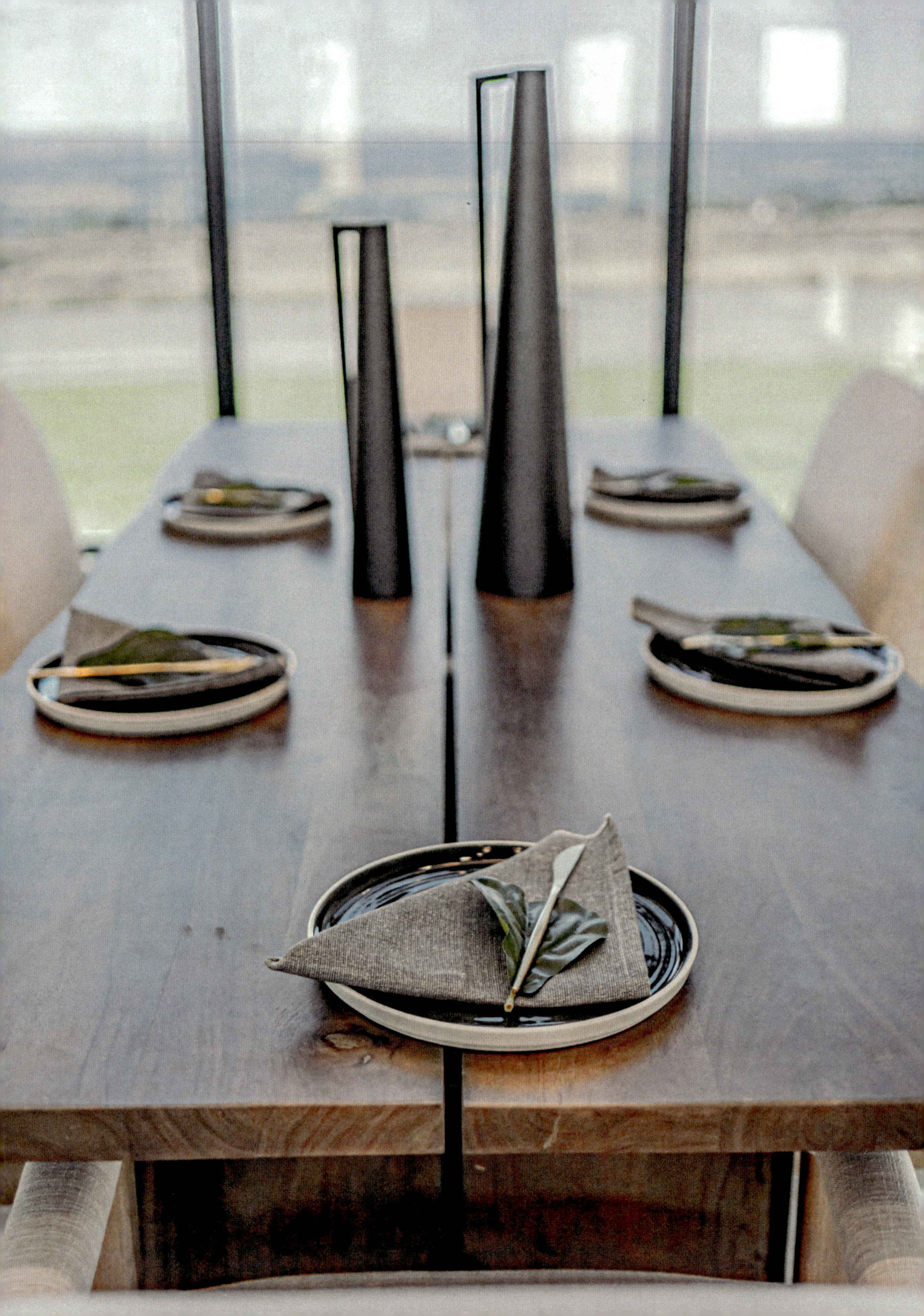

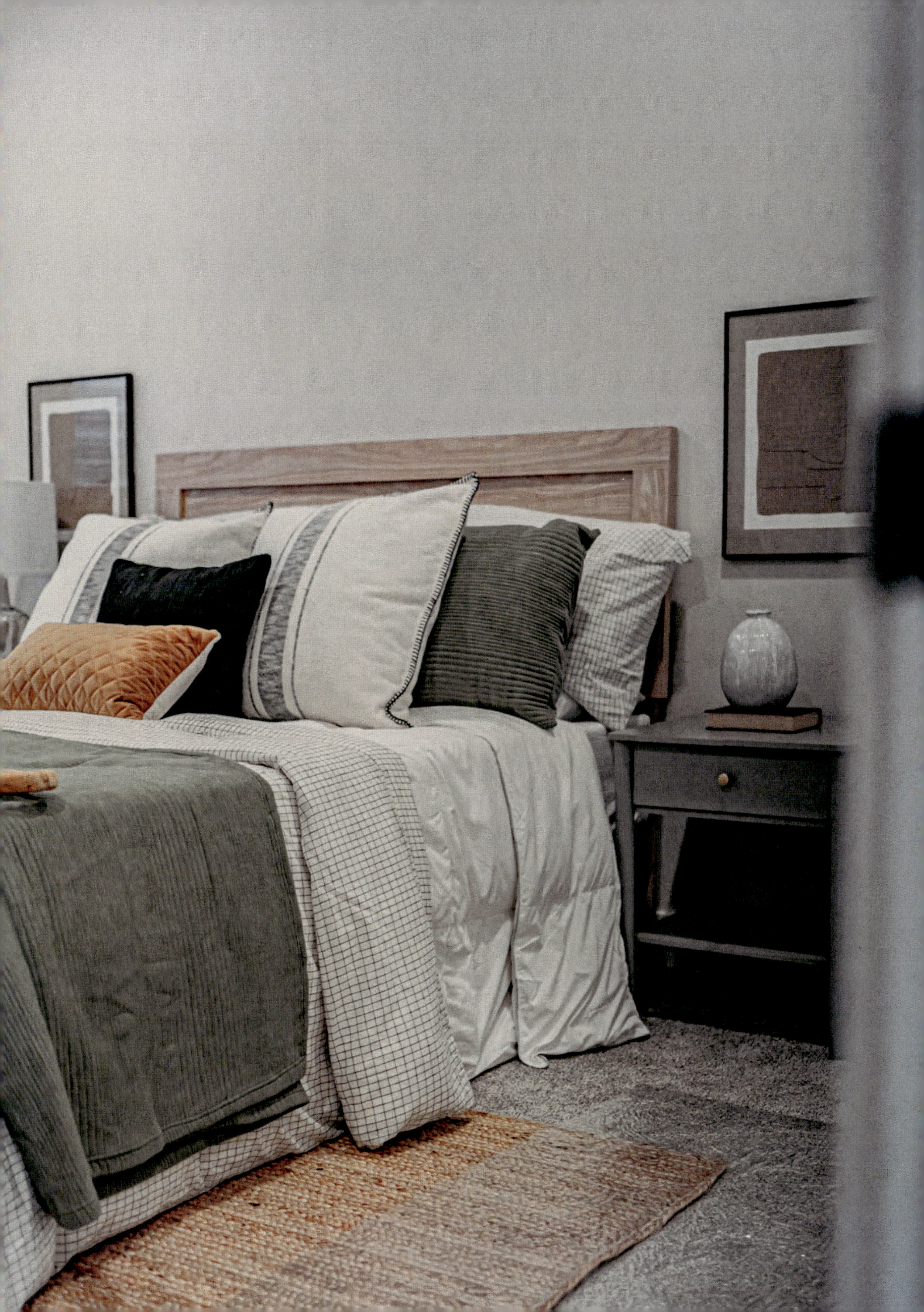

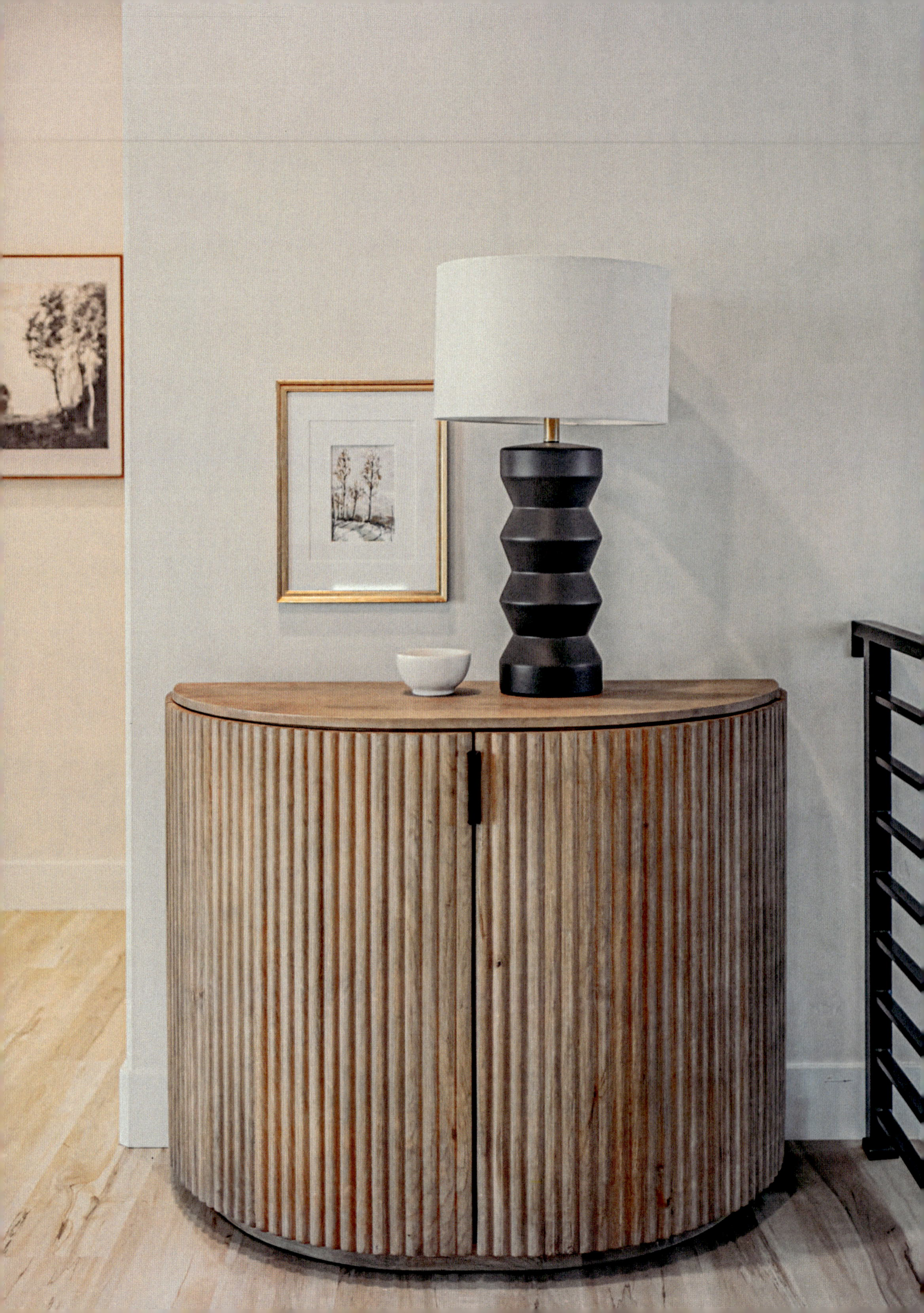

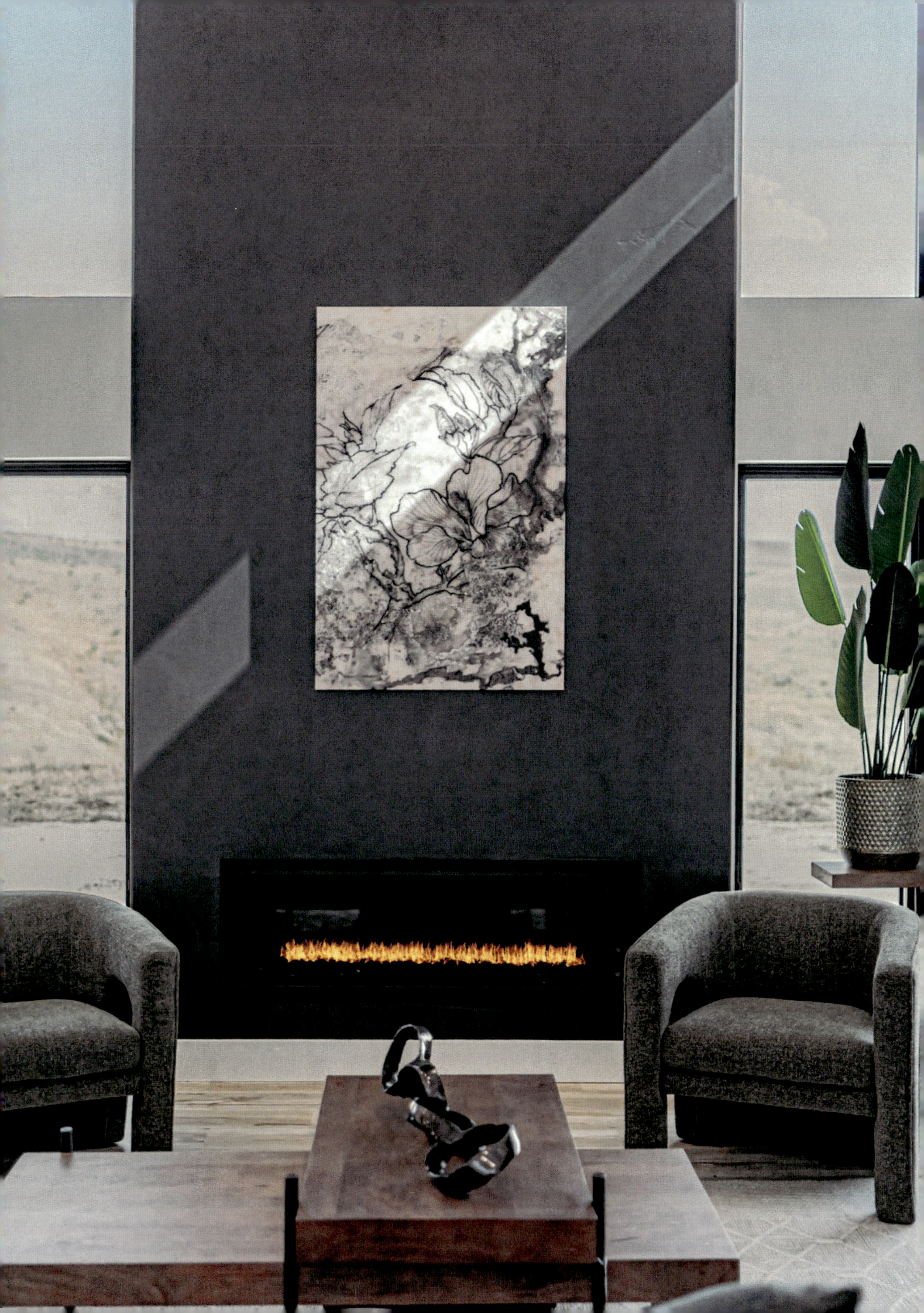

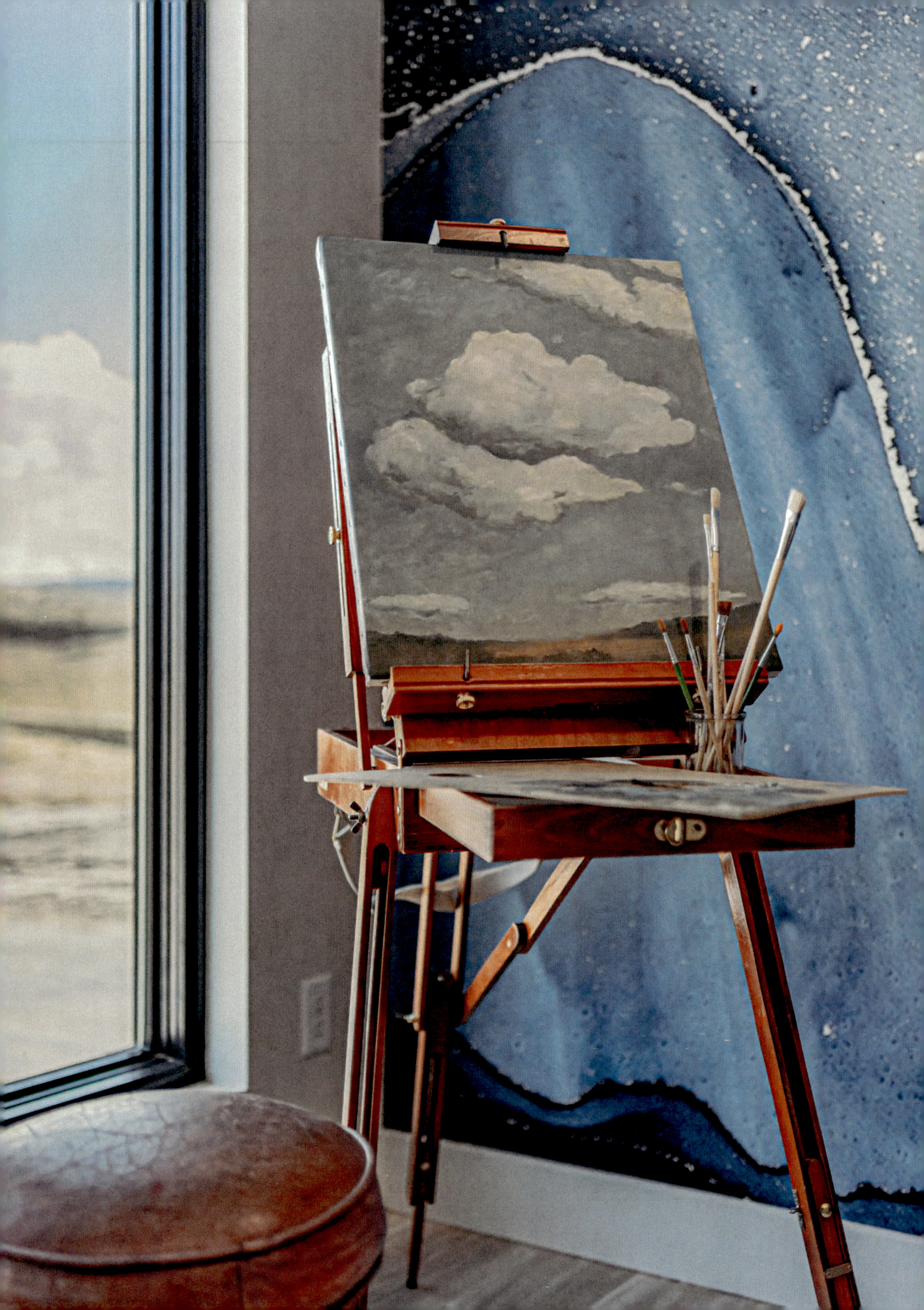

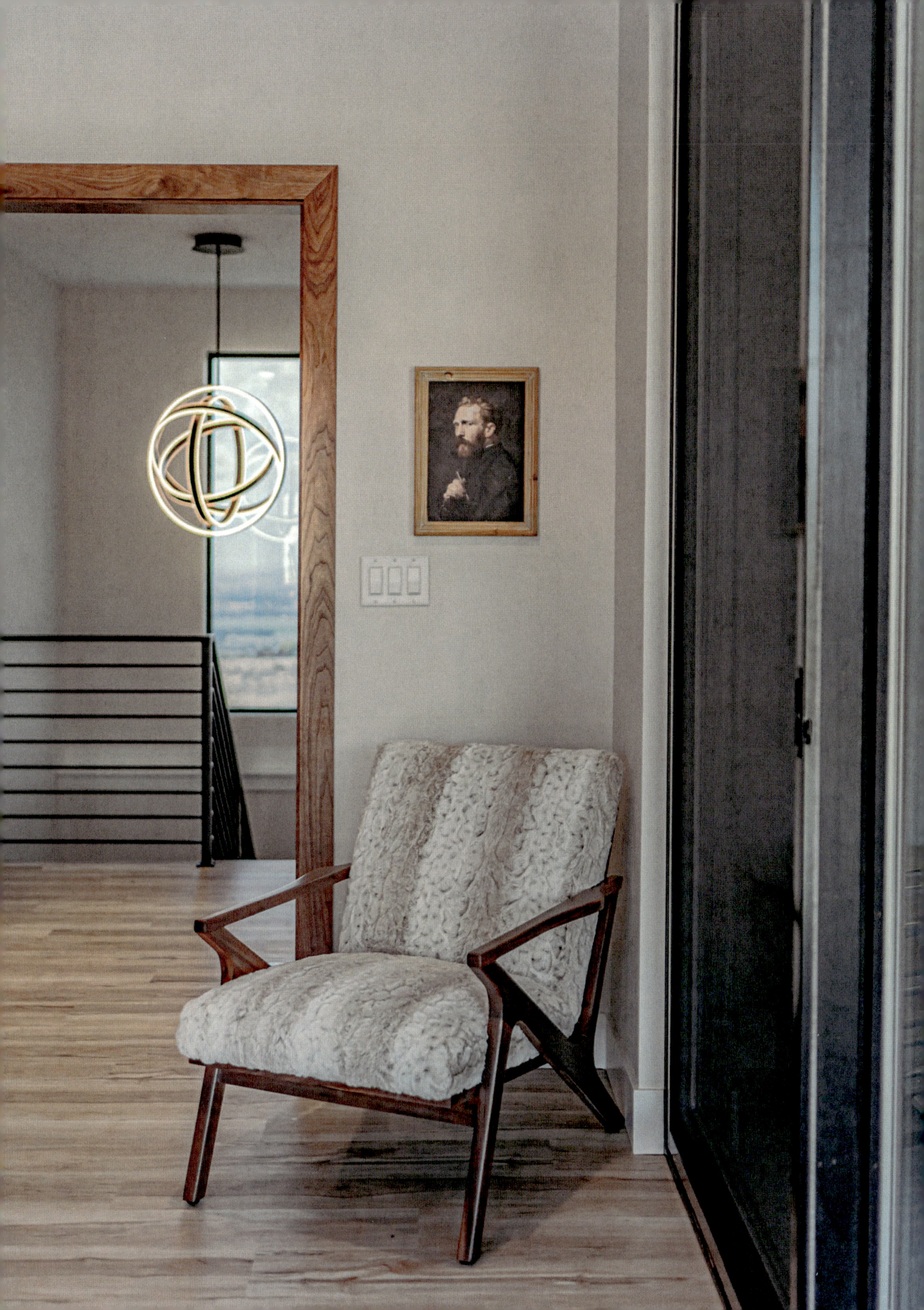

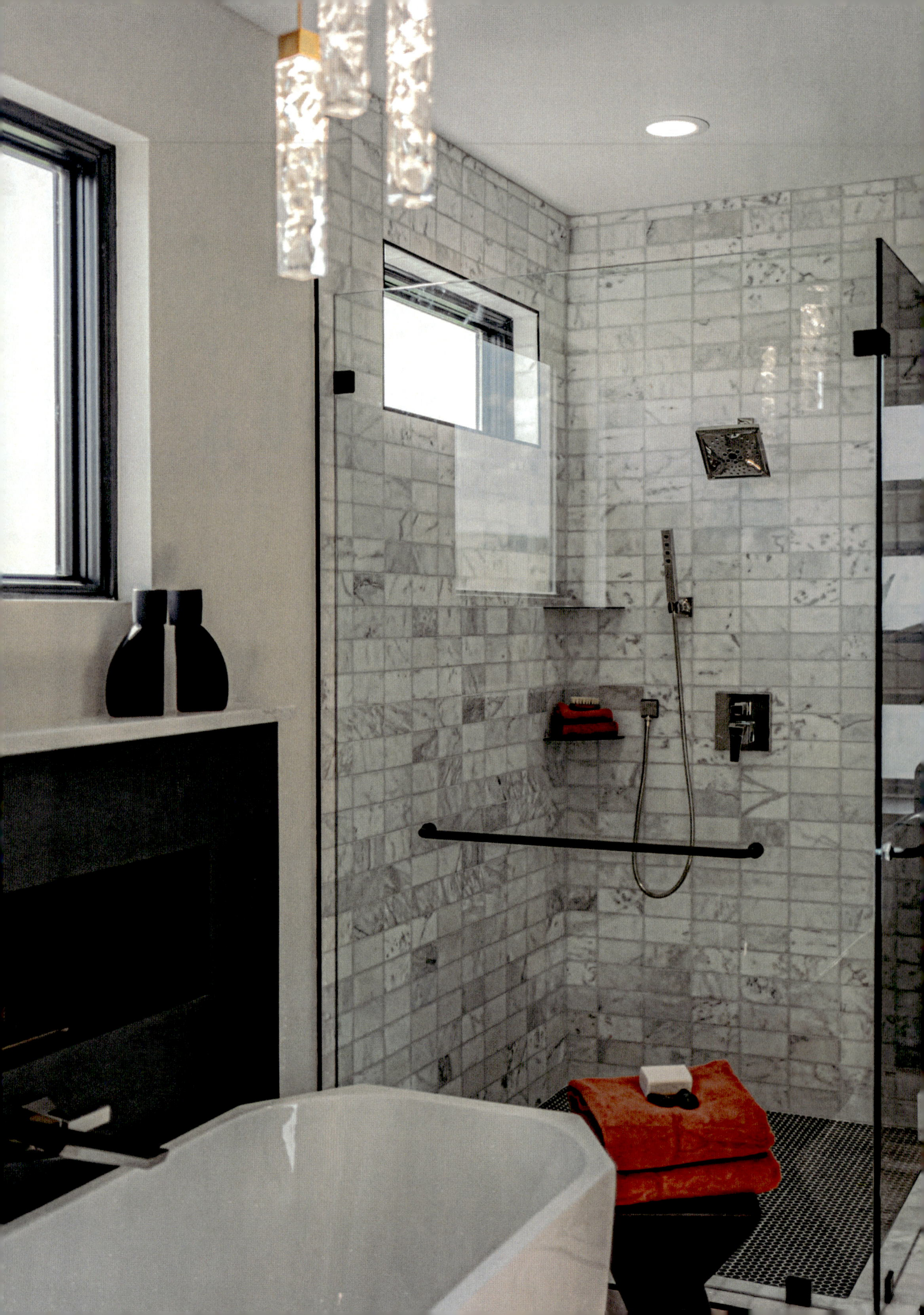

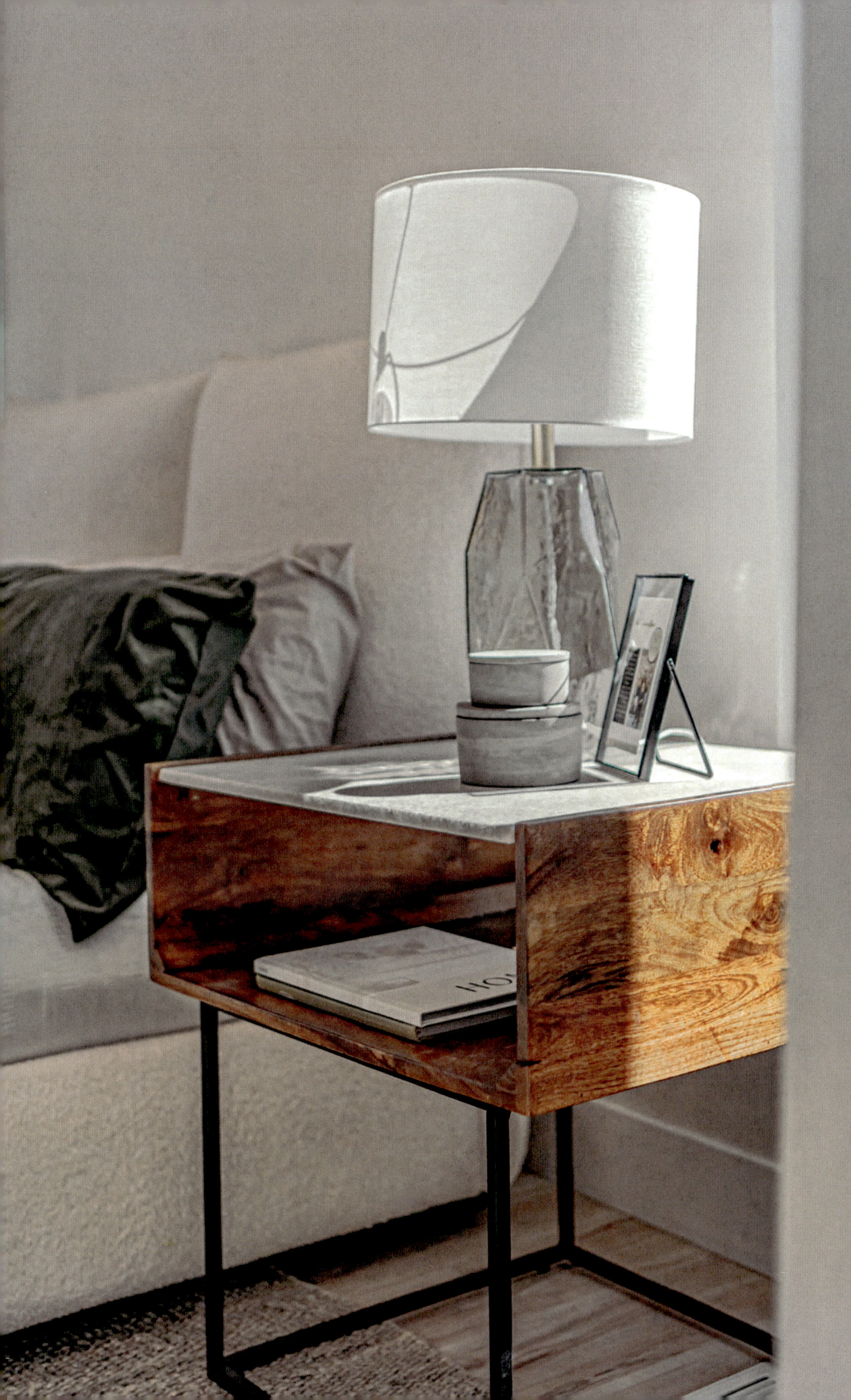

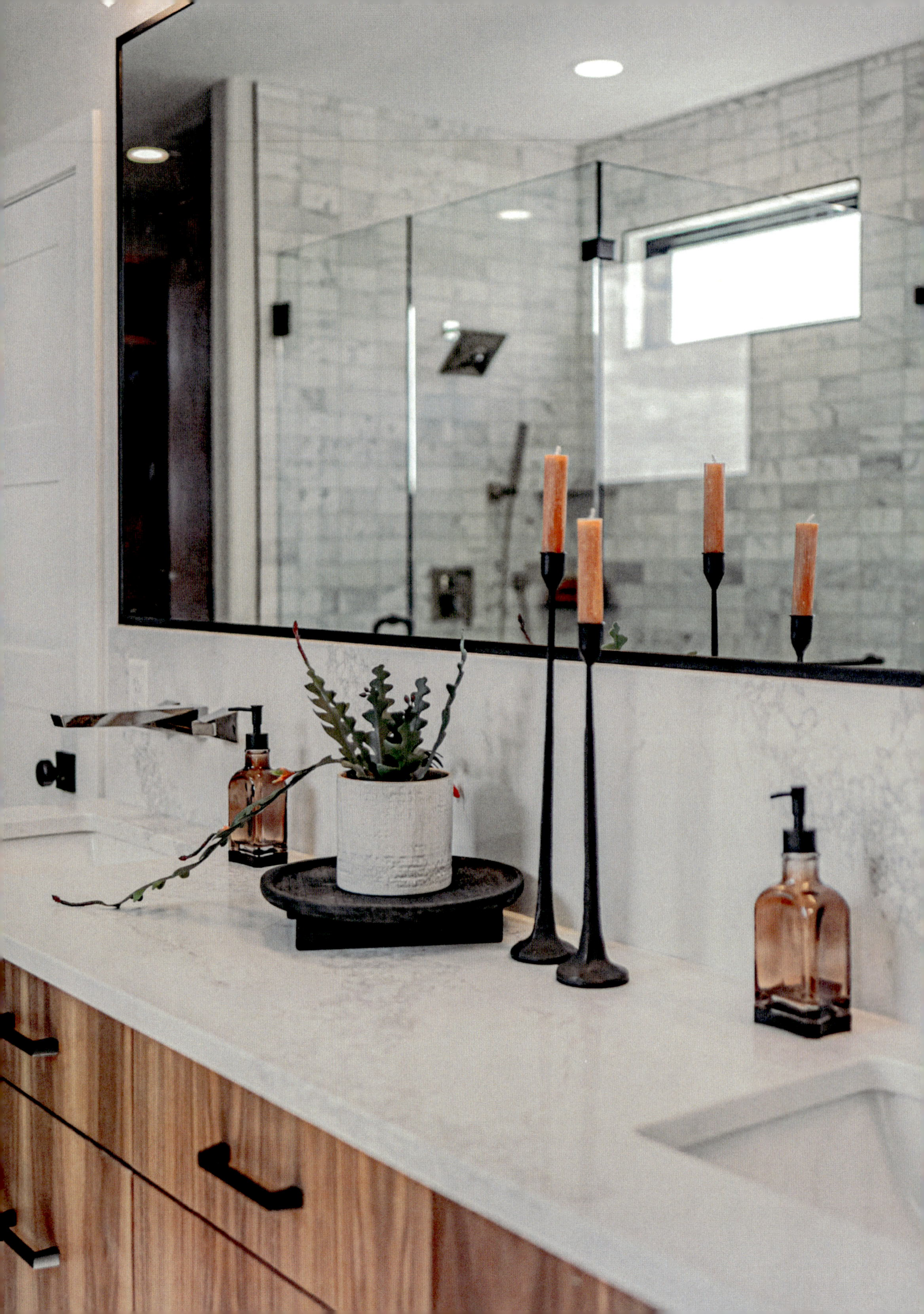

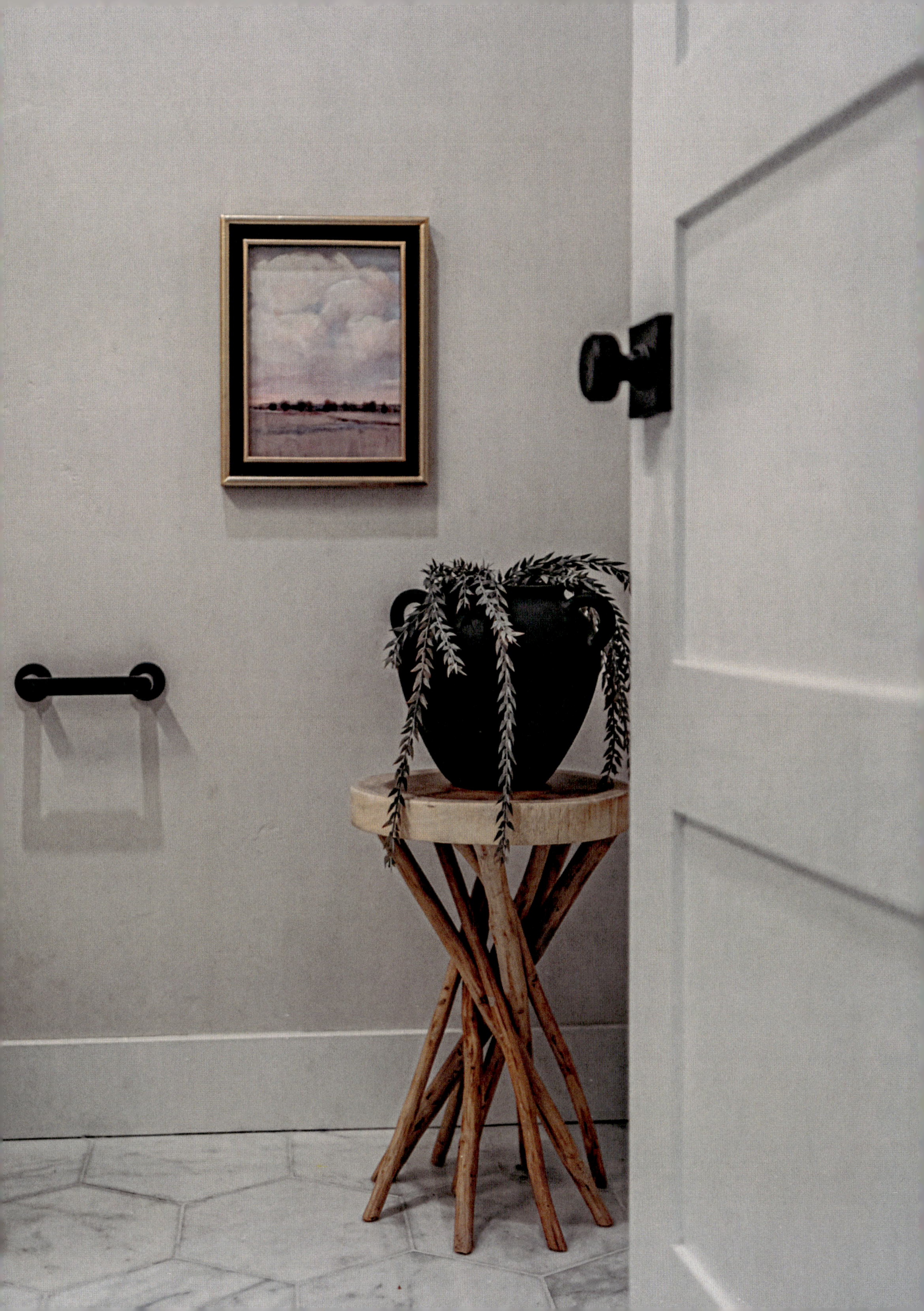

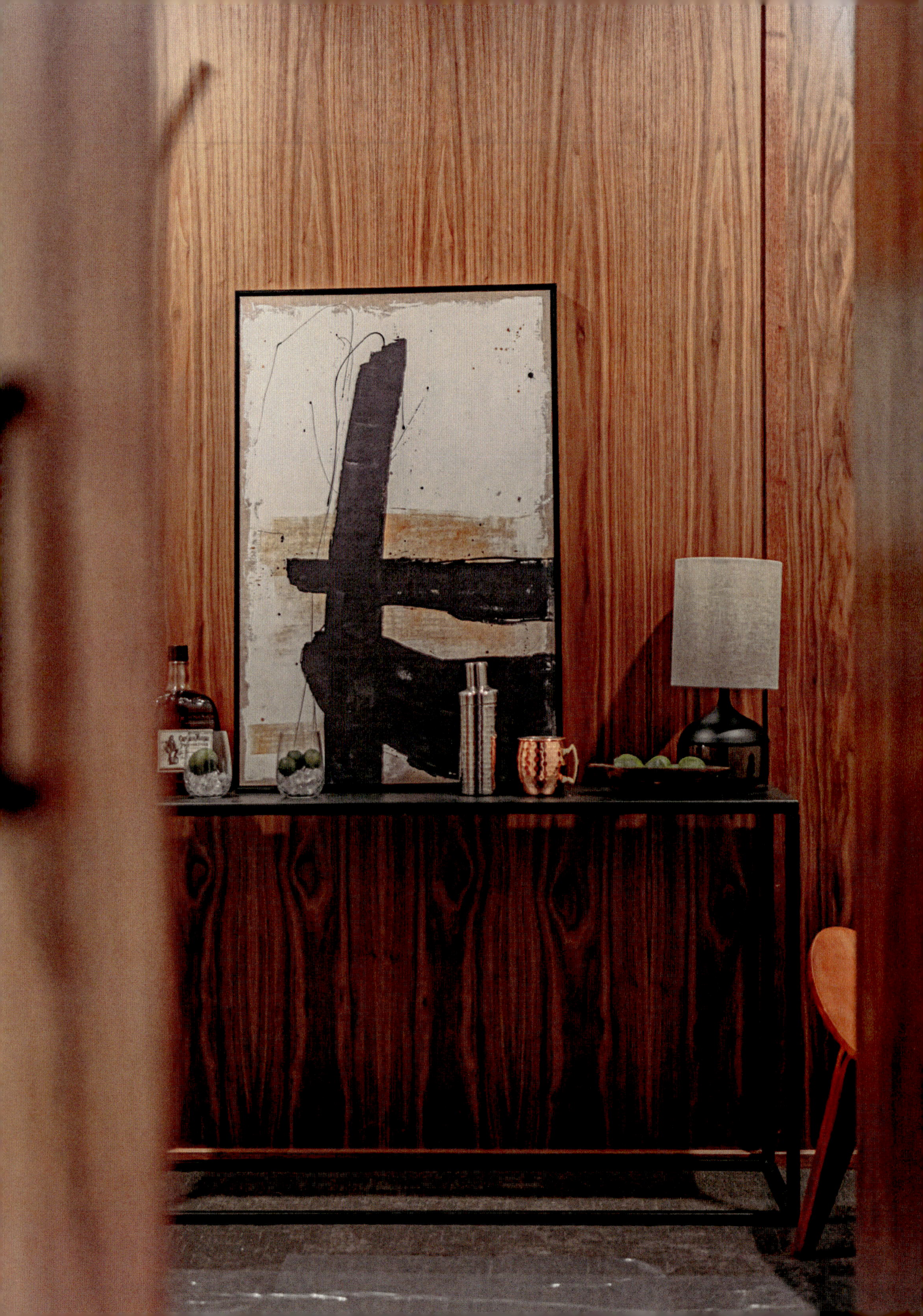

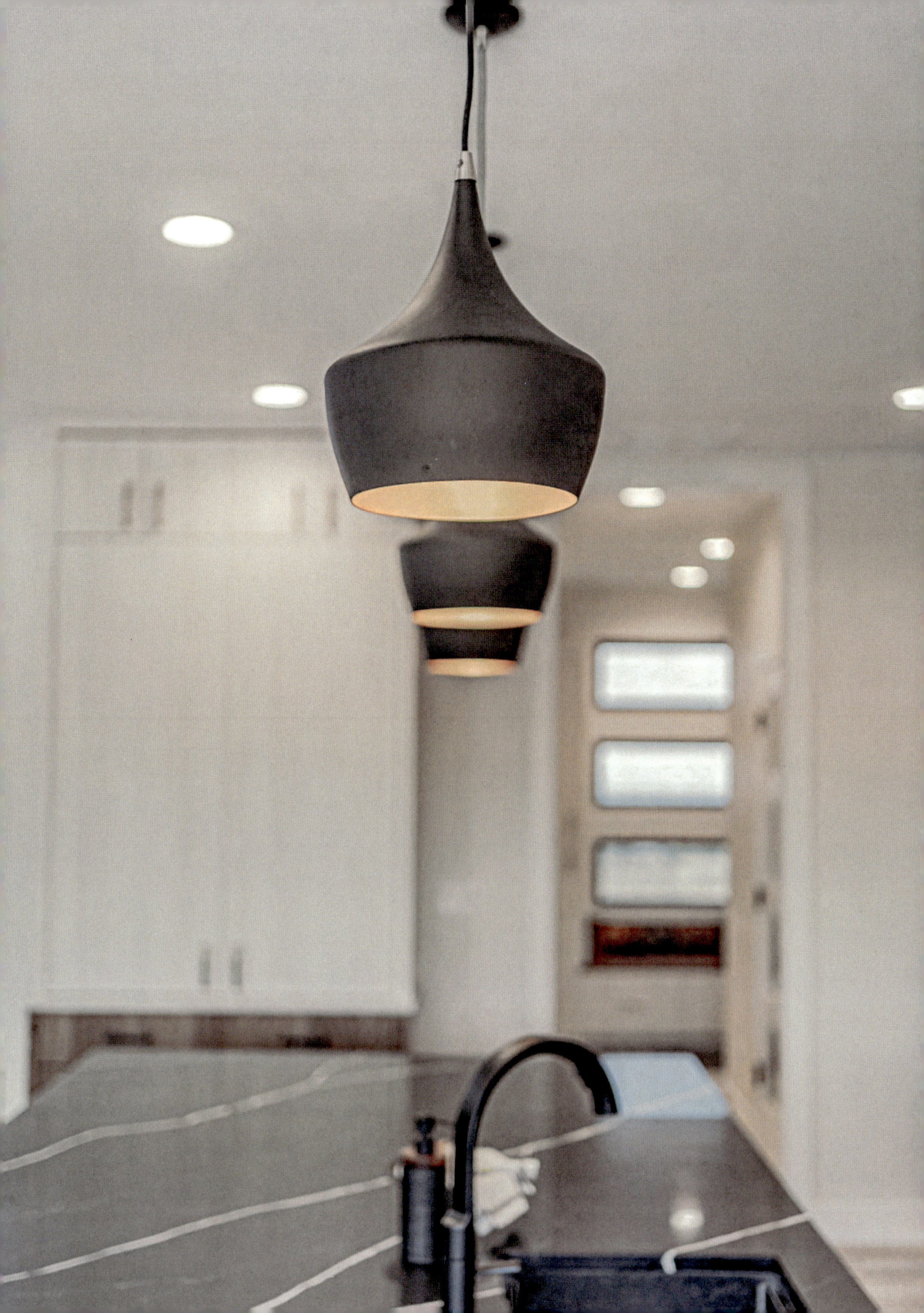

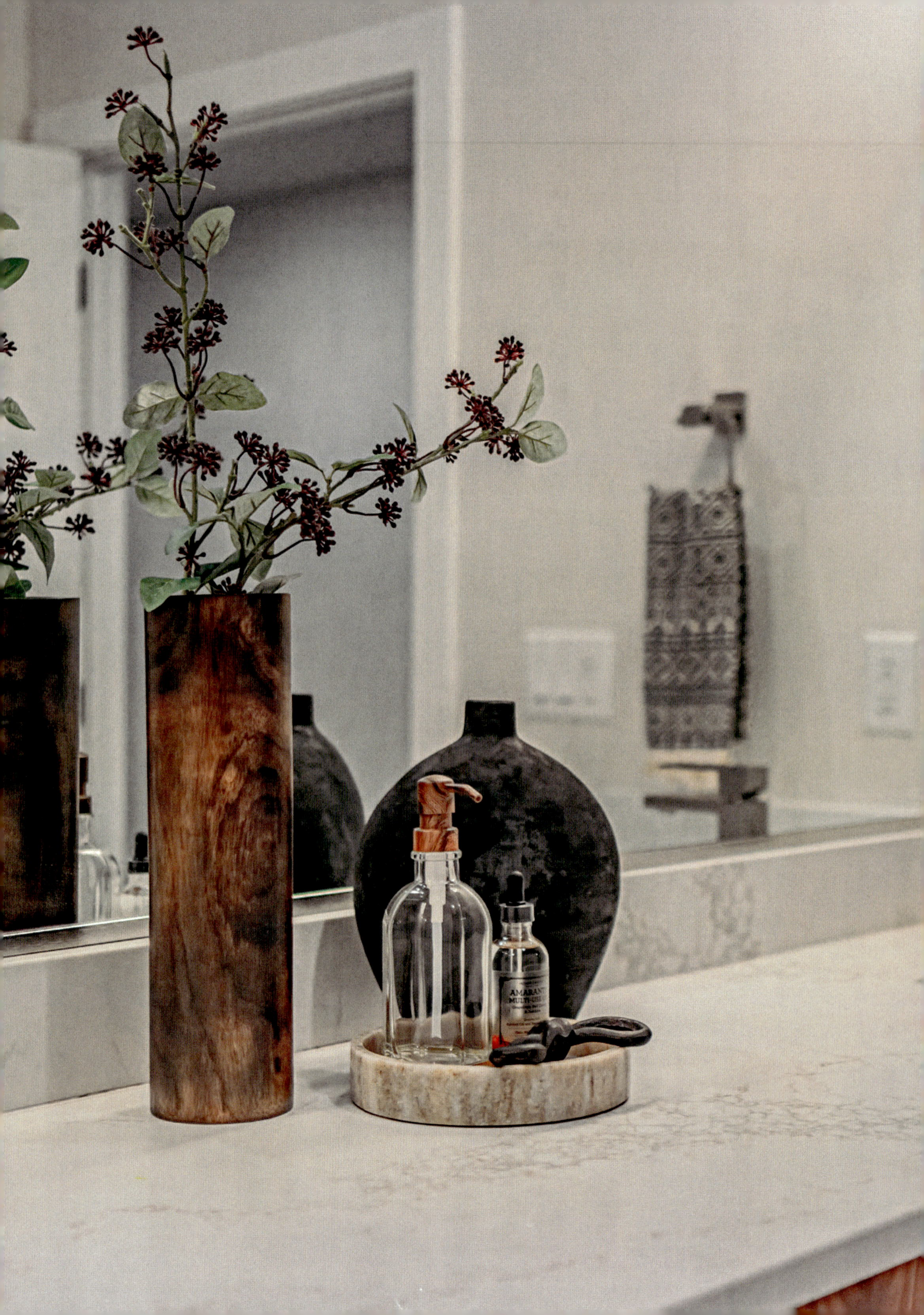

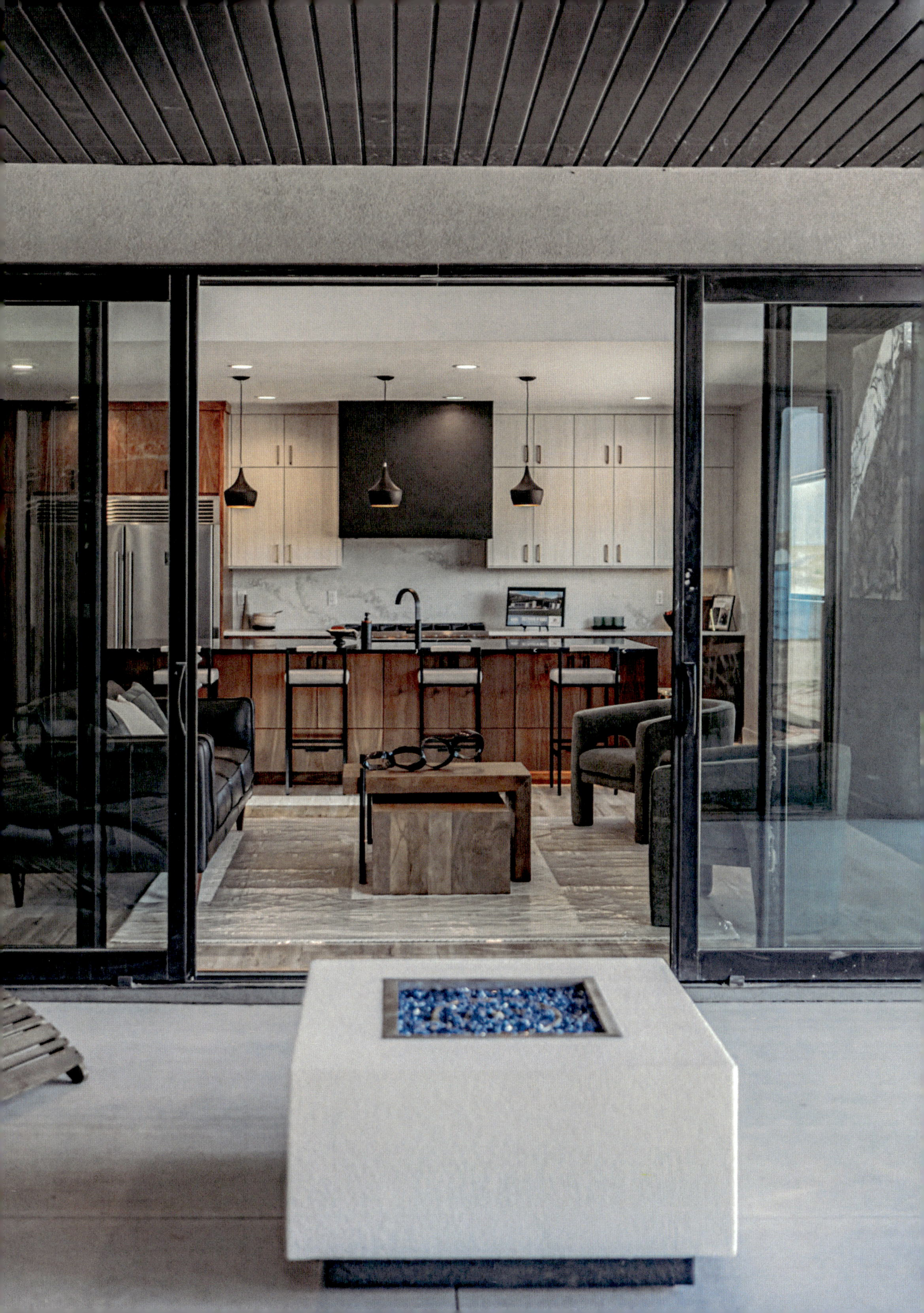

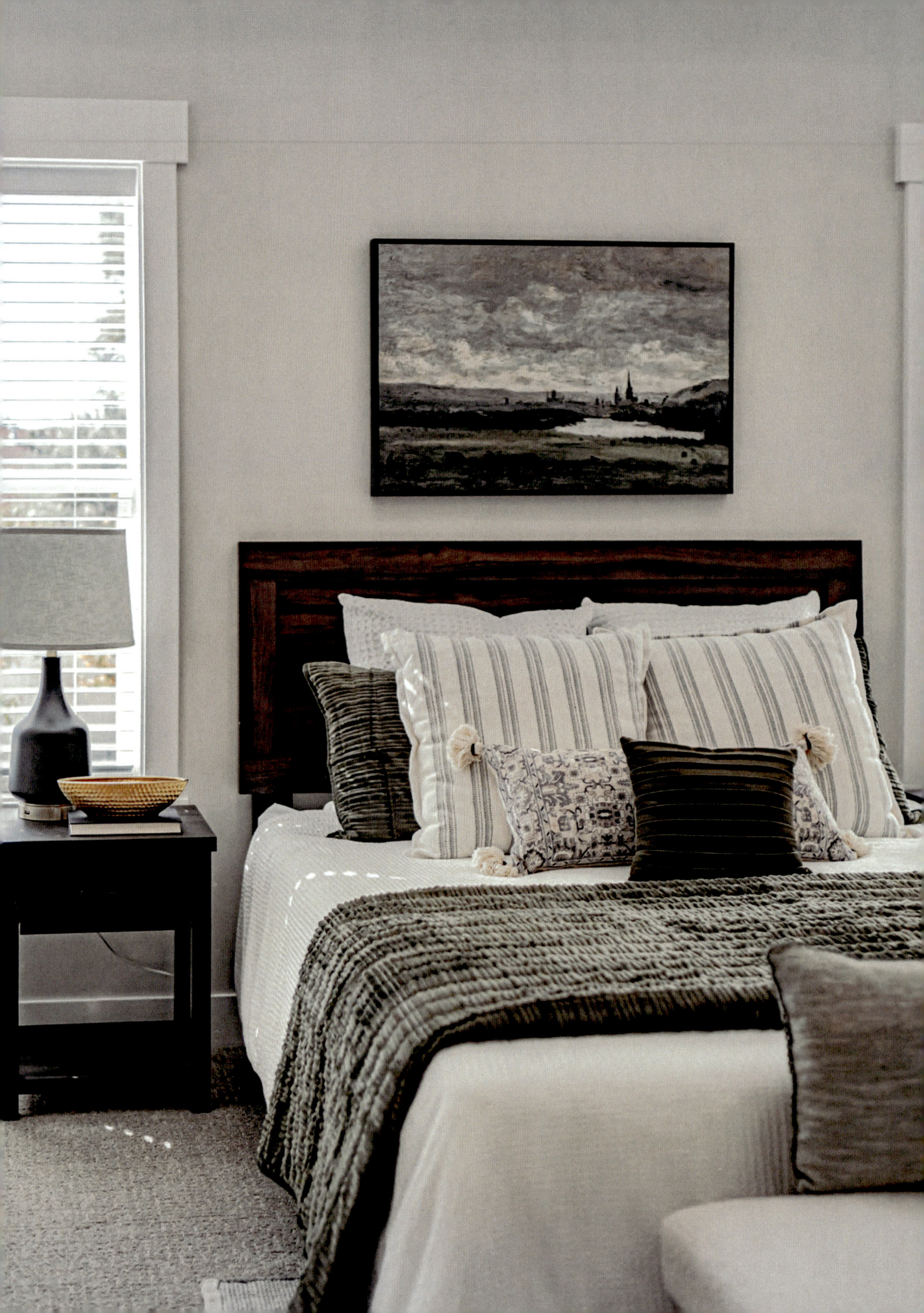

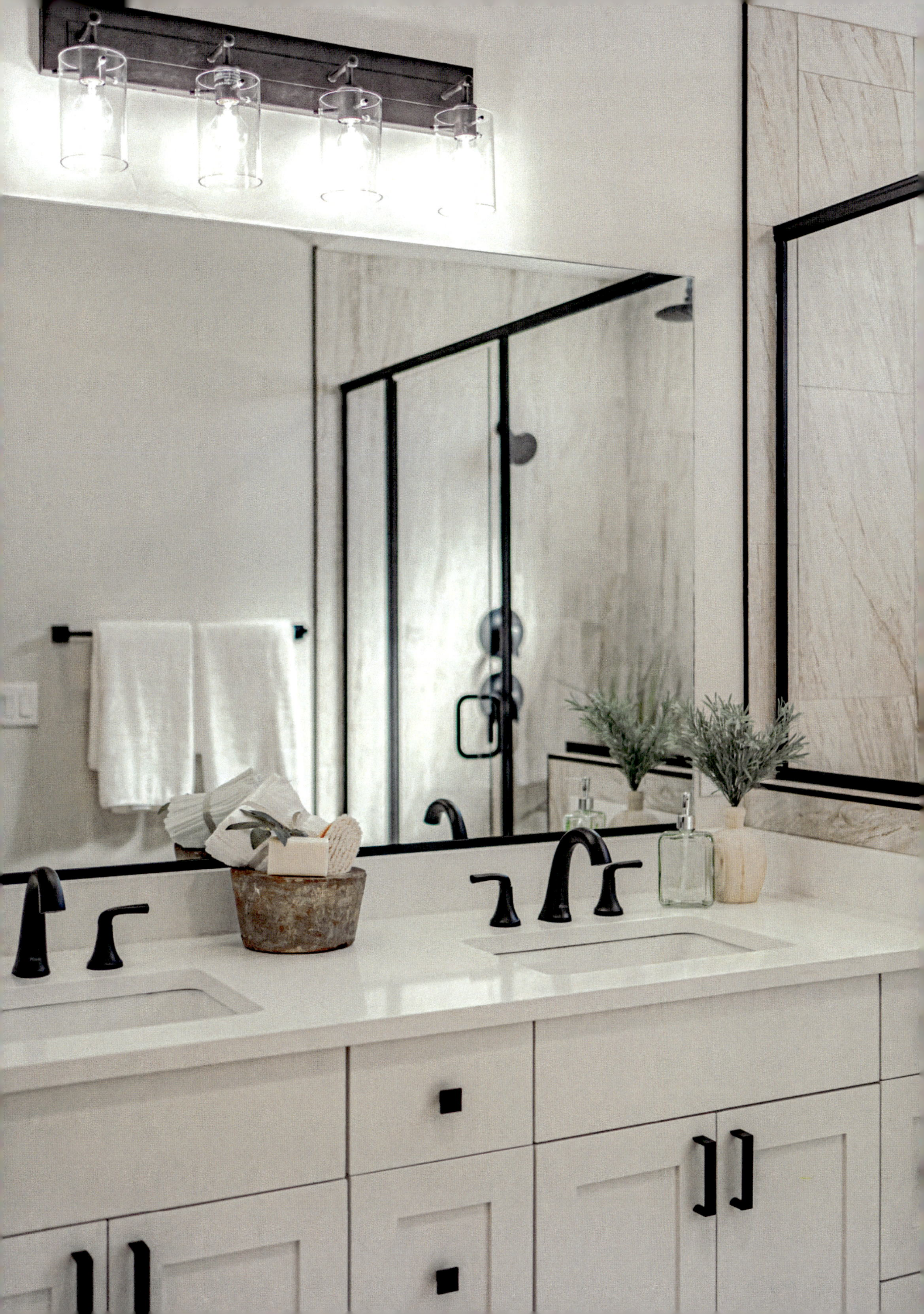

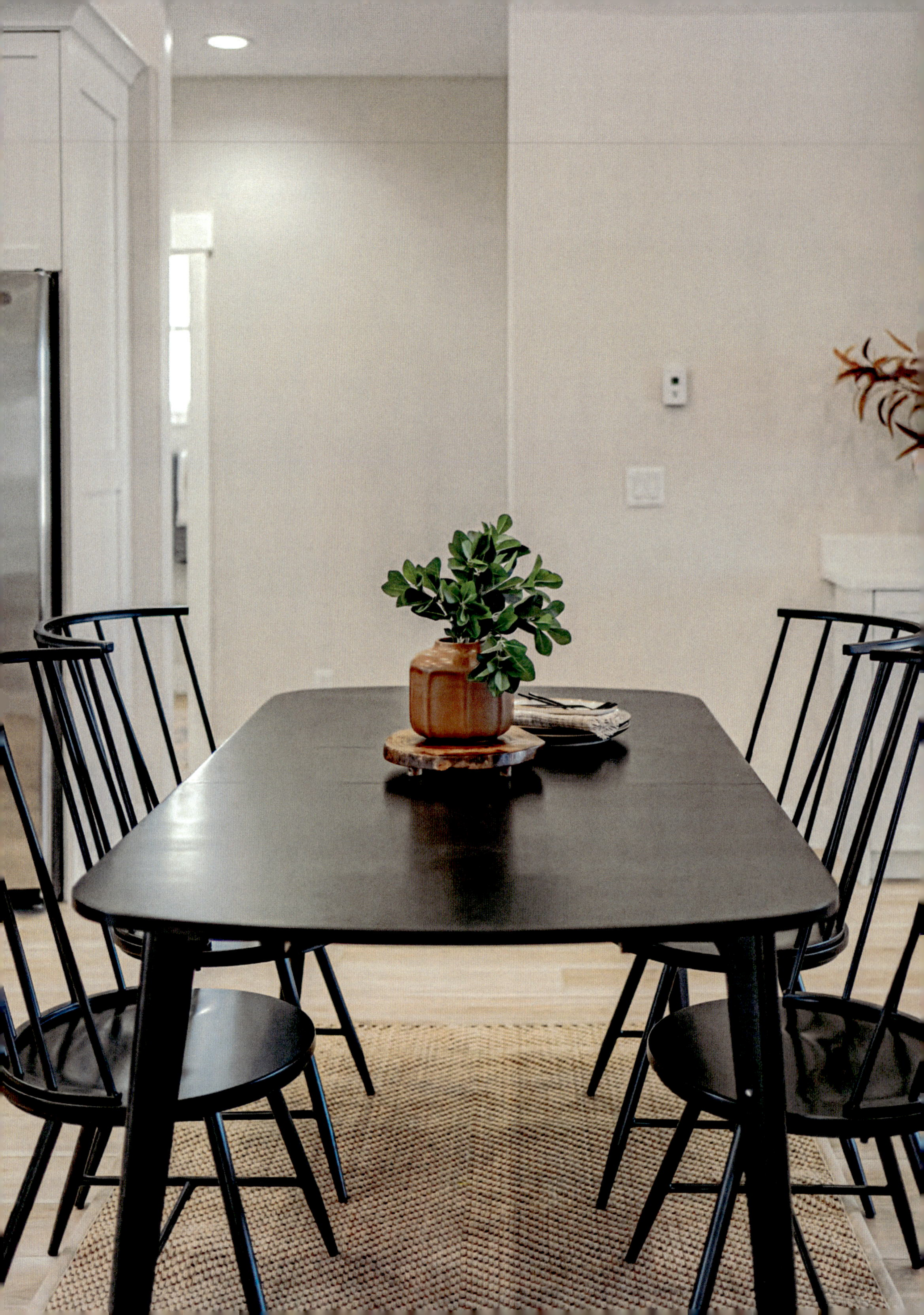

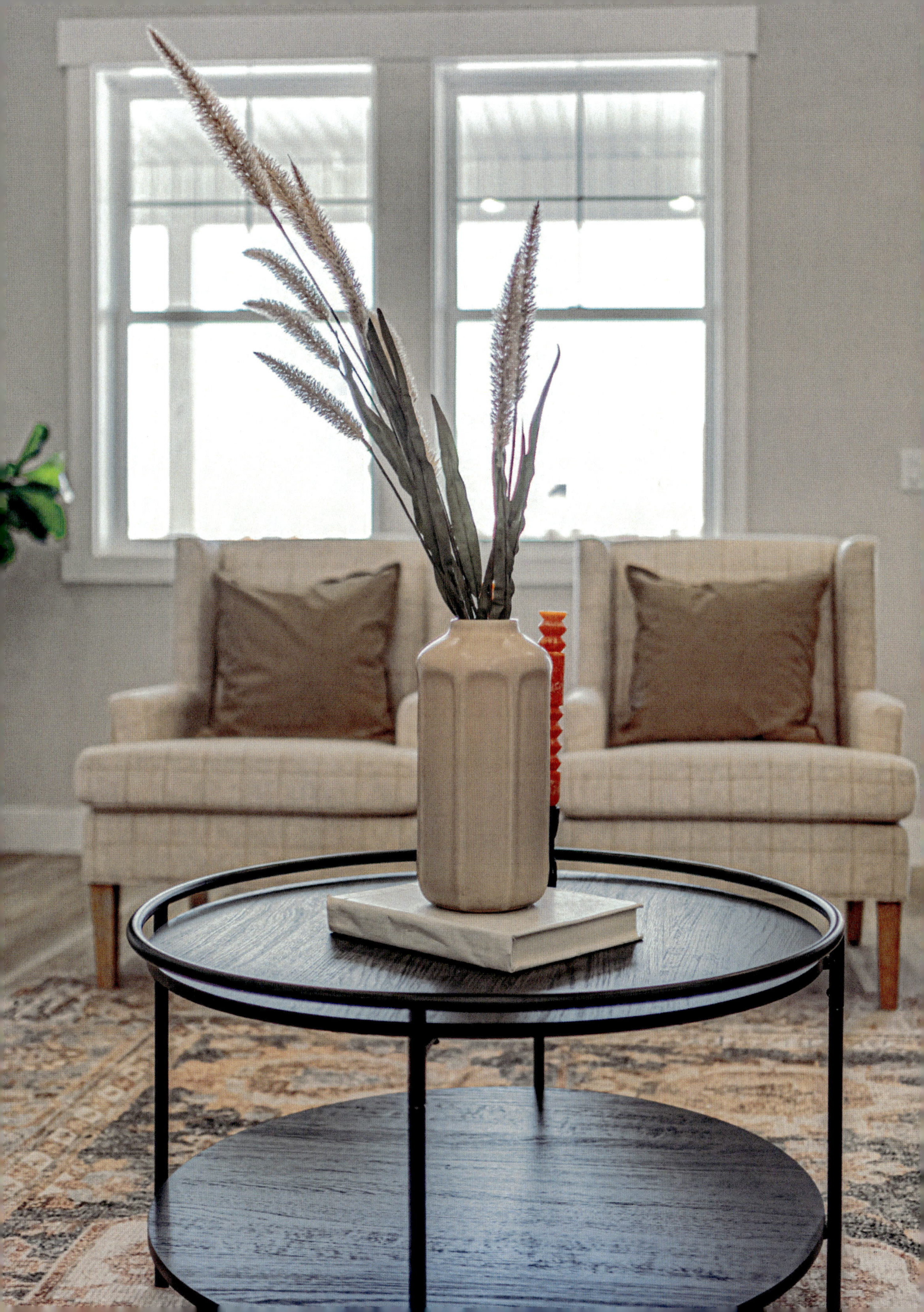

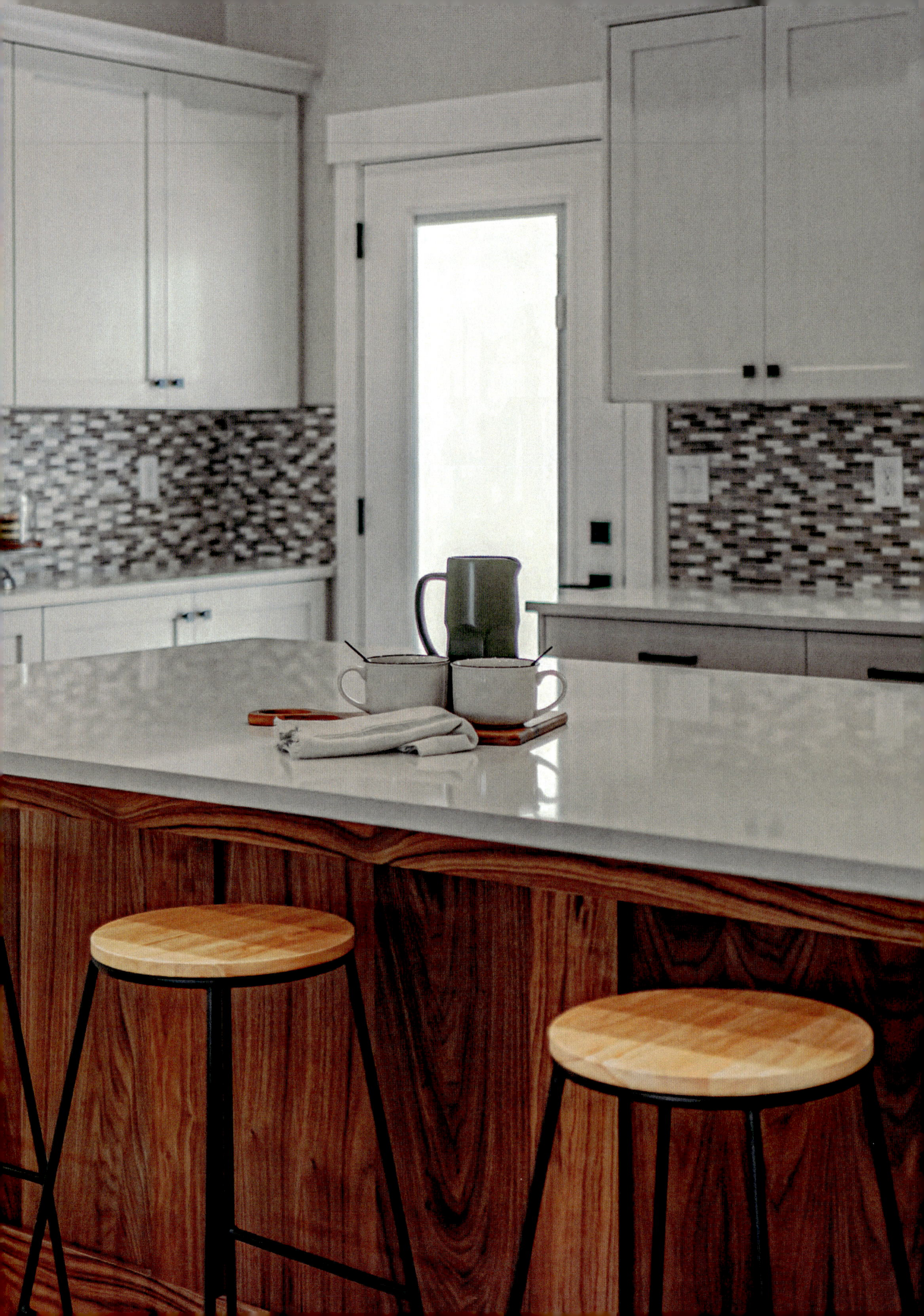

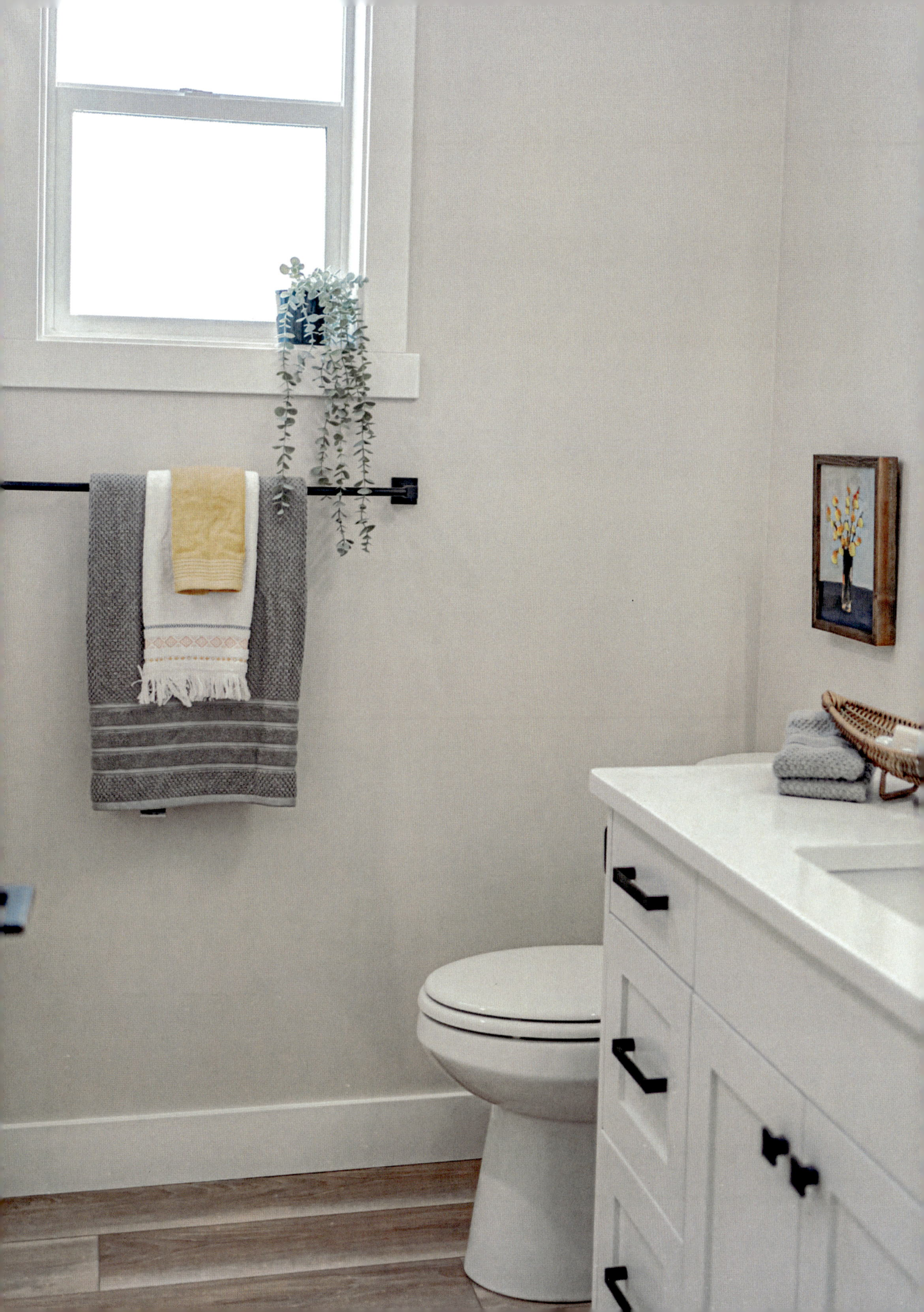

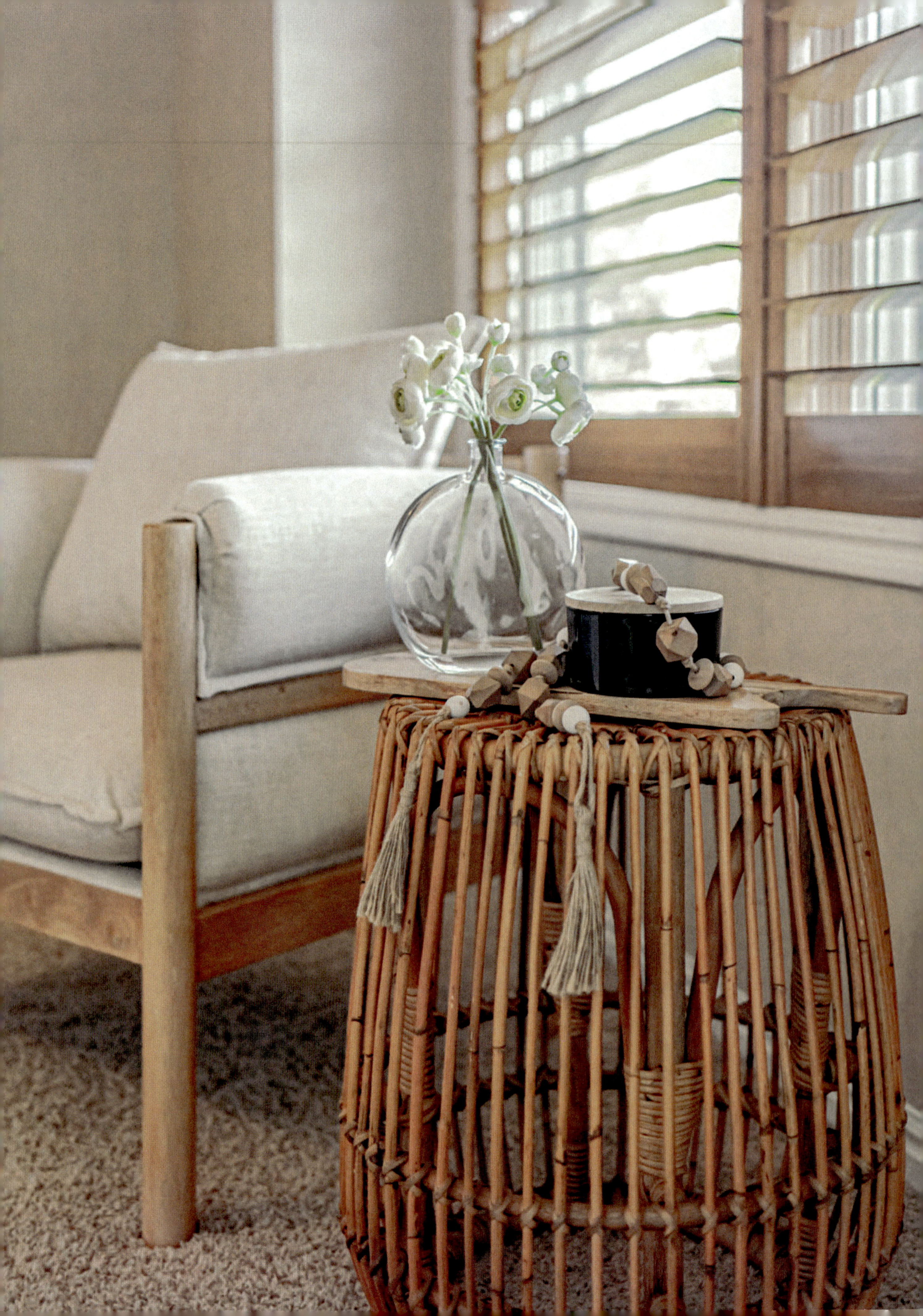

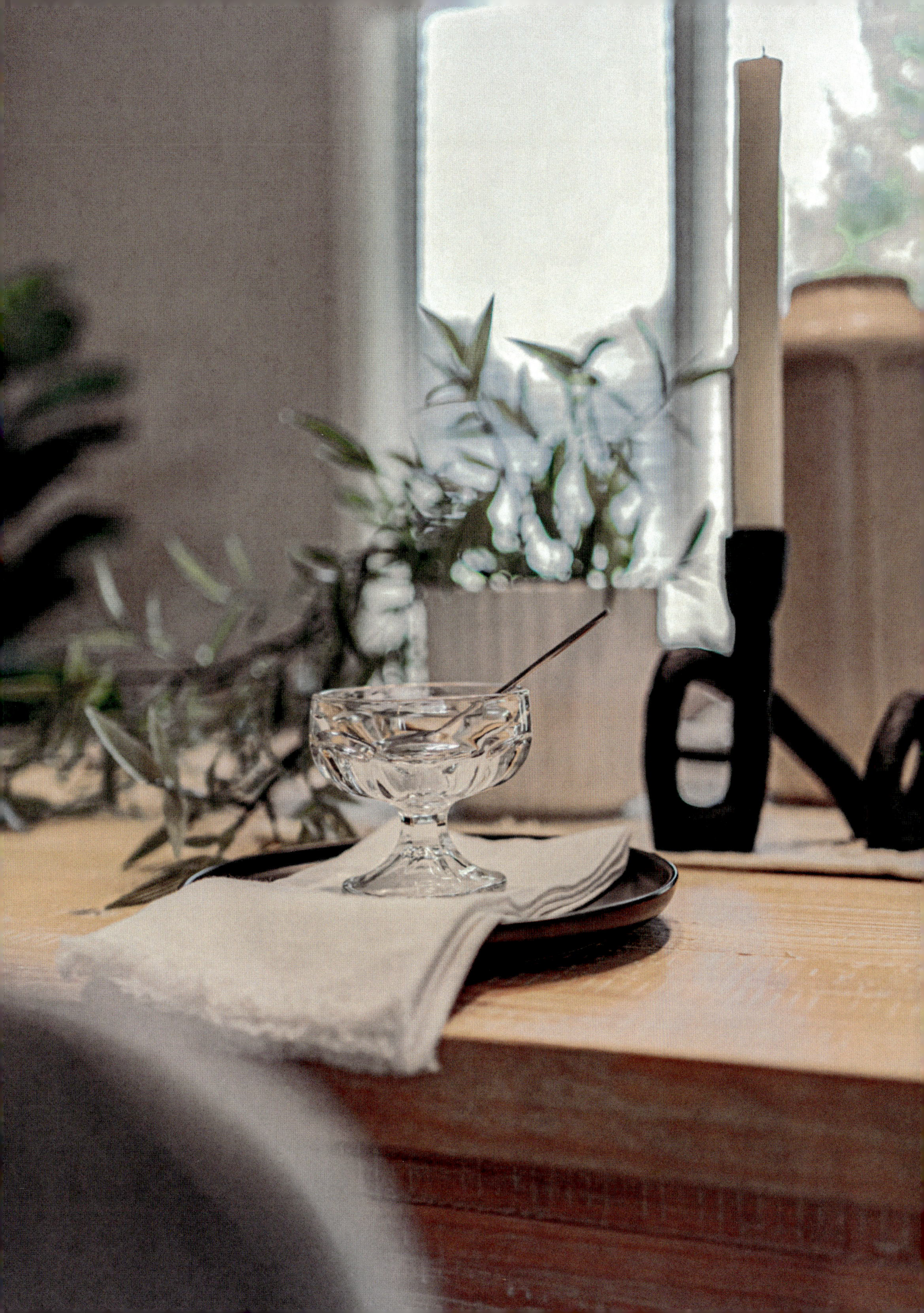

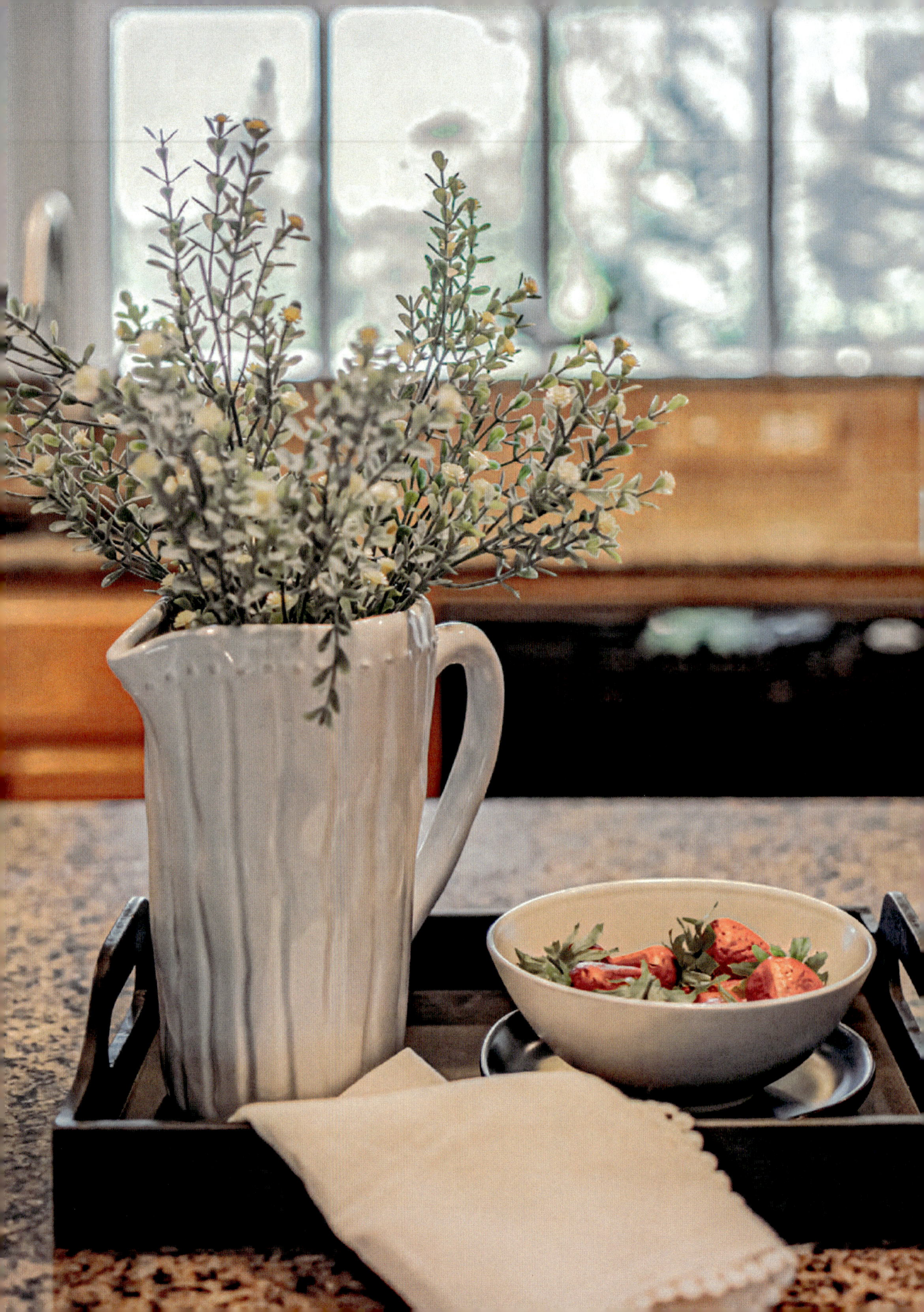

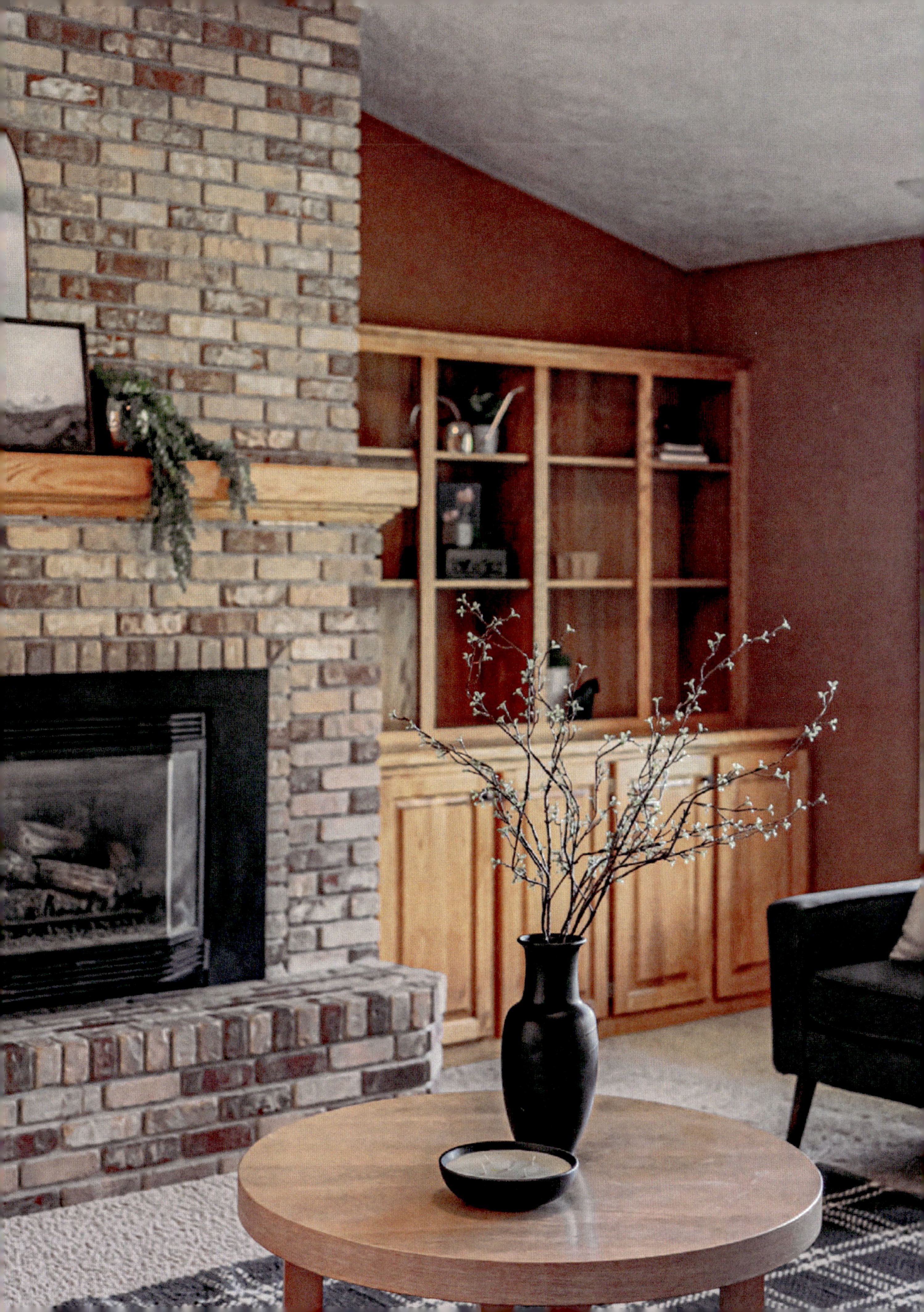

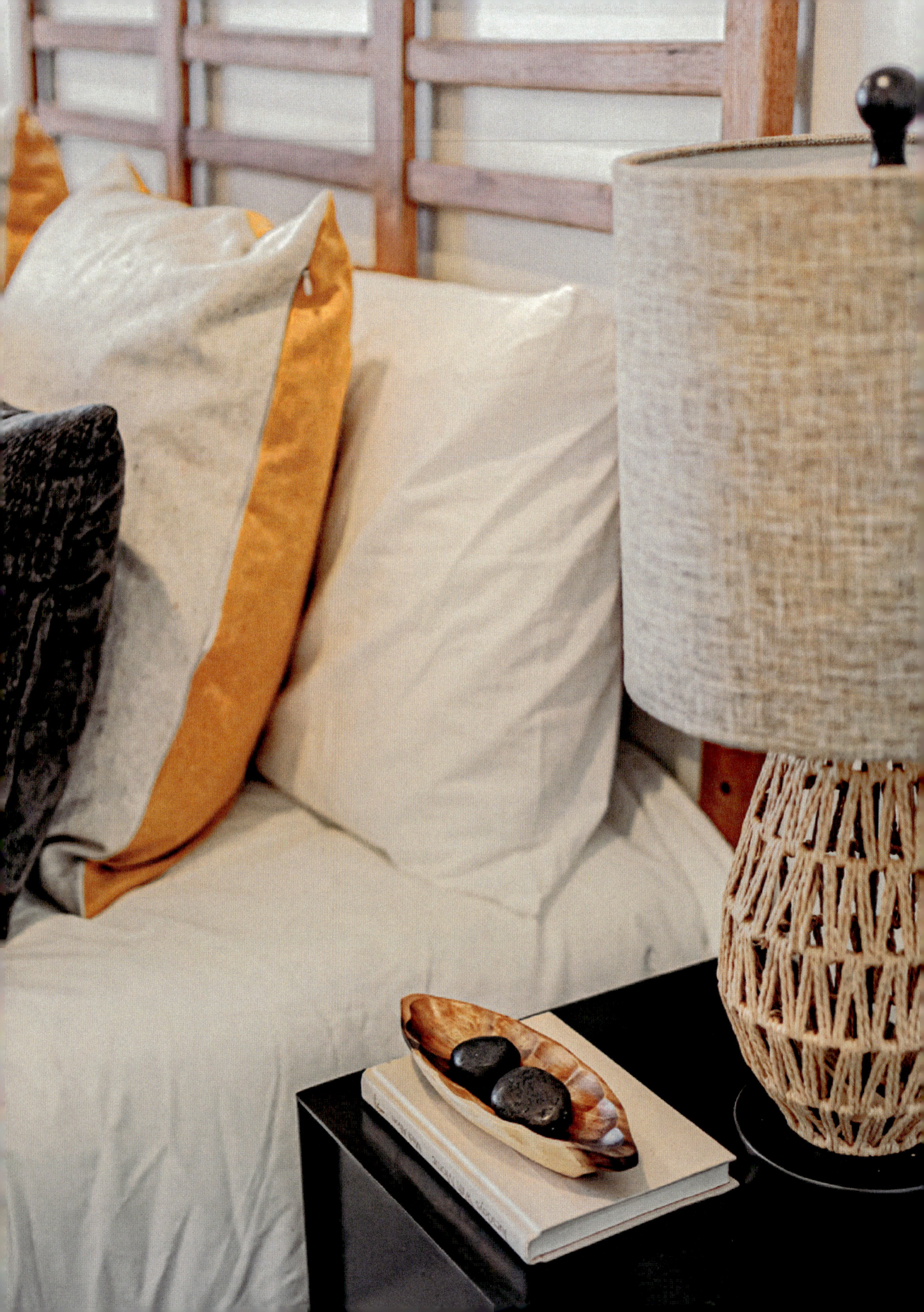

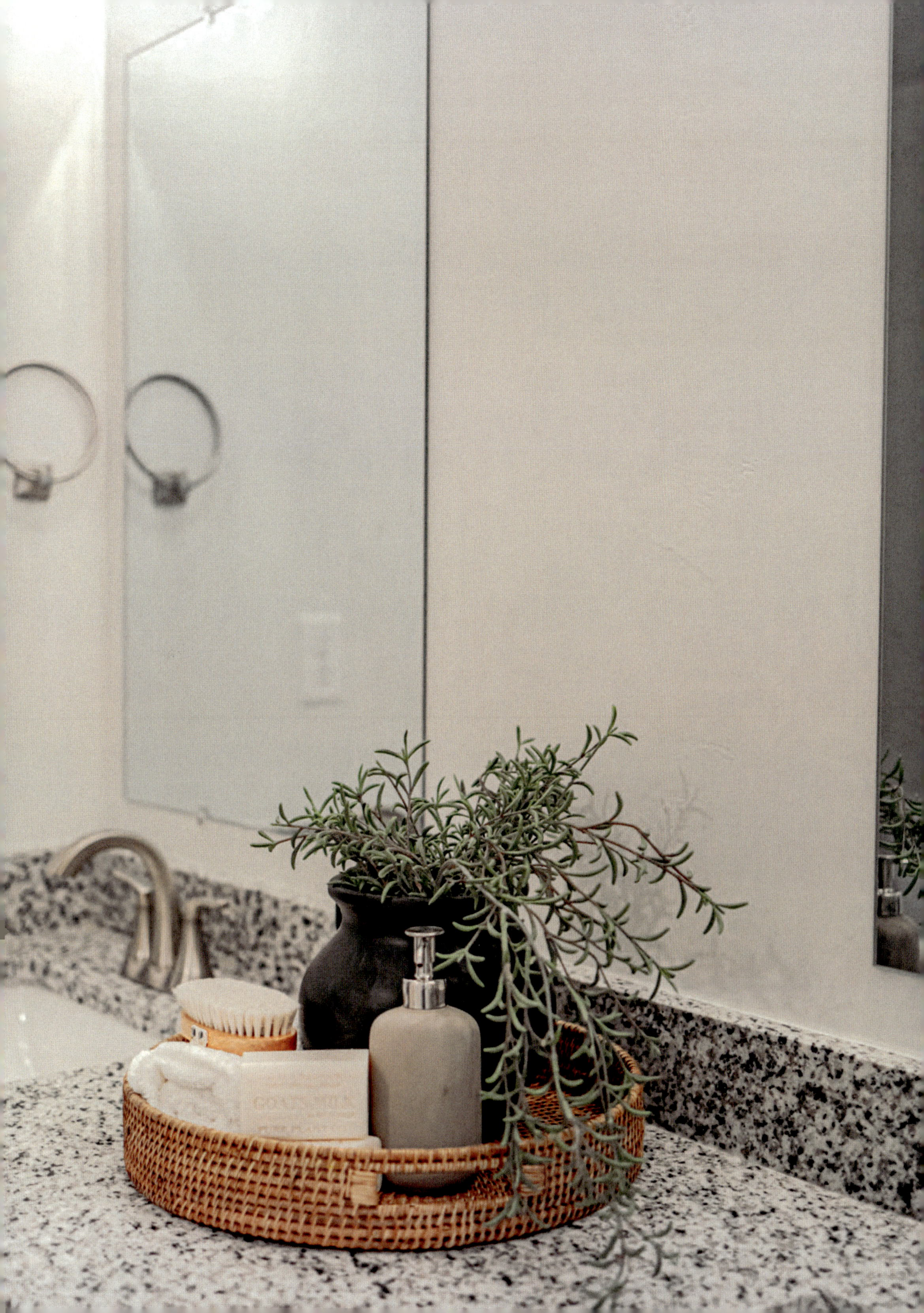

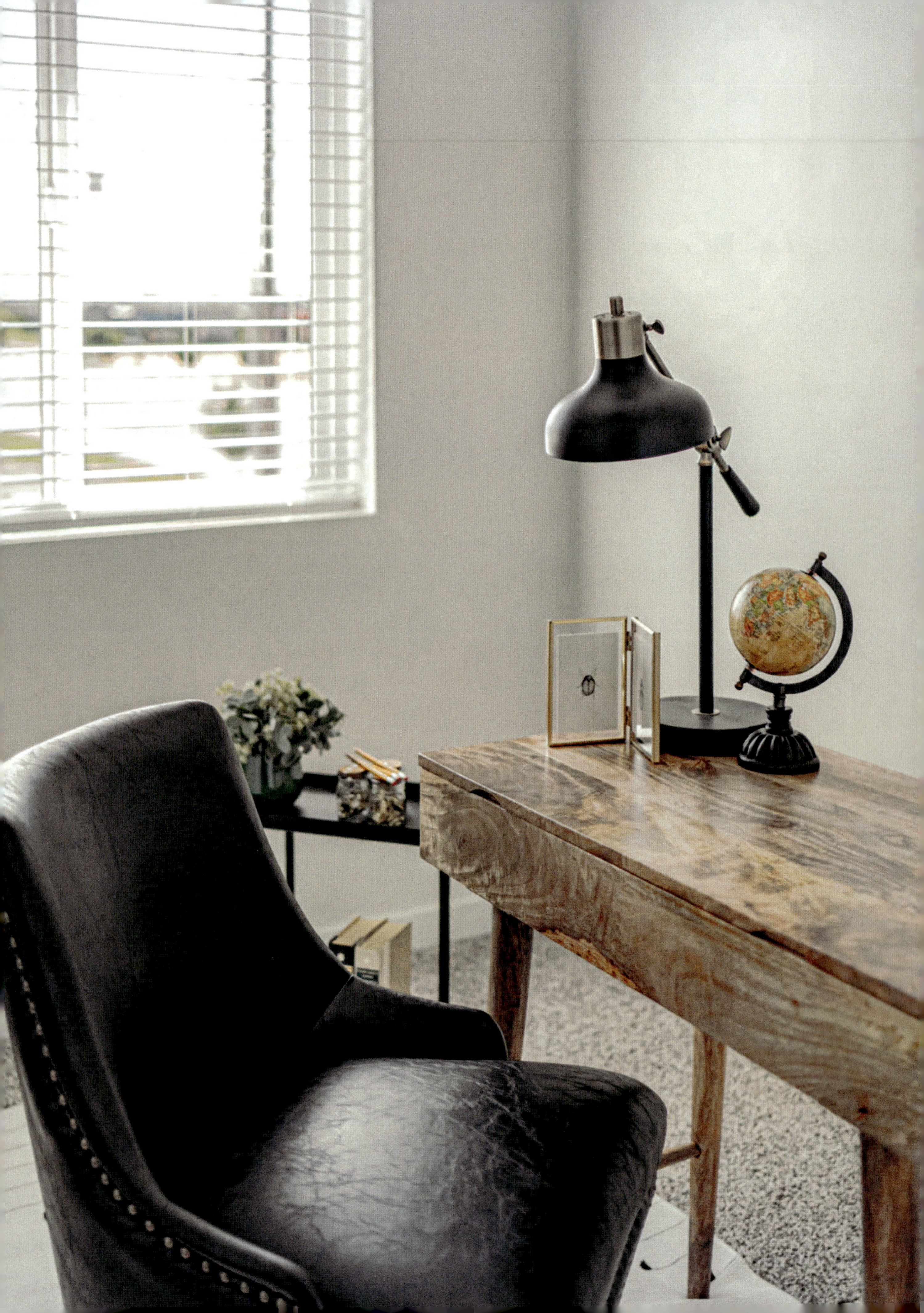

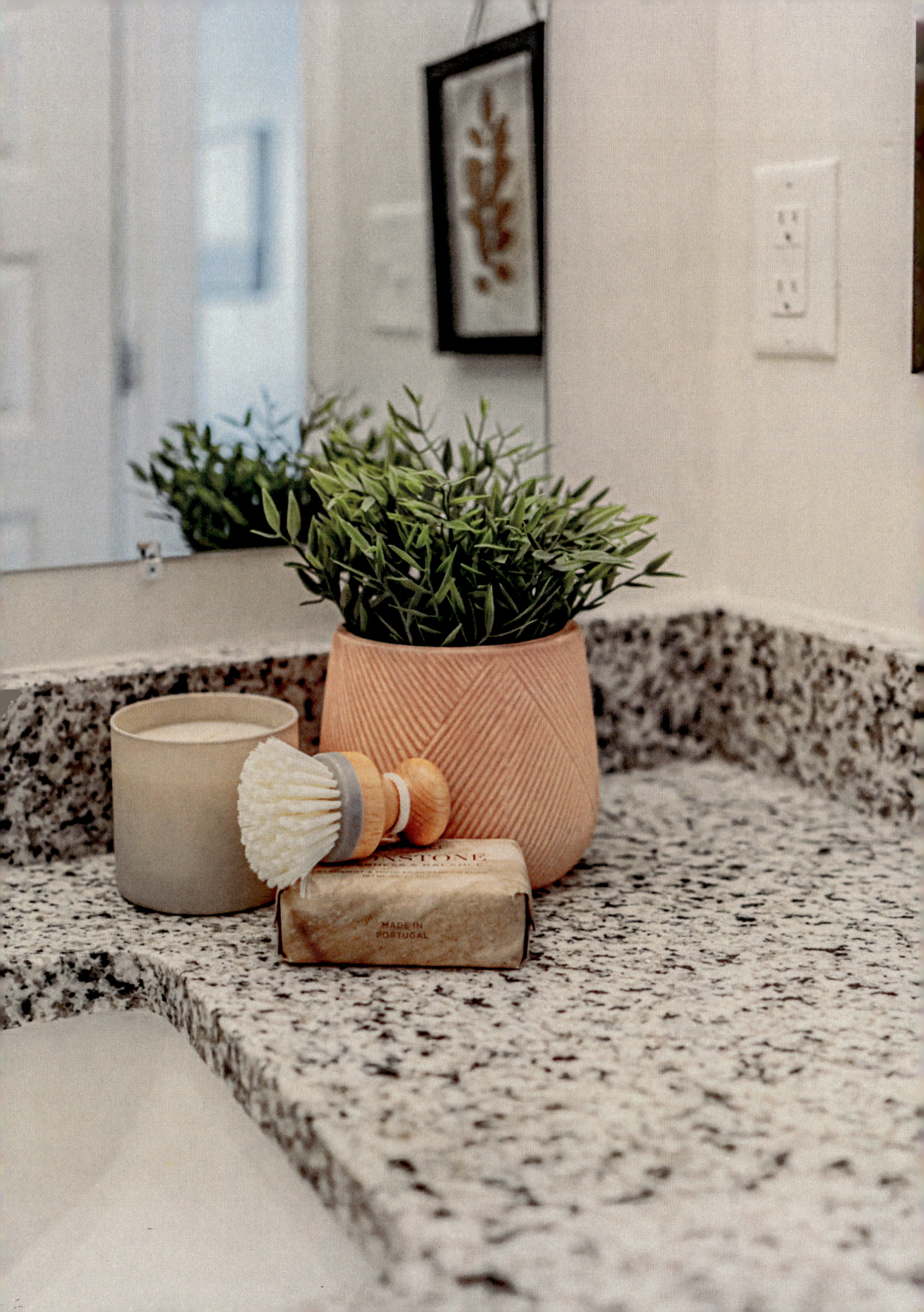
MADE IN
PORTUGAL

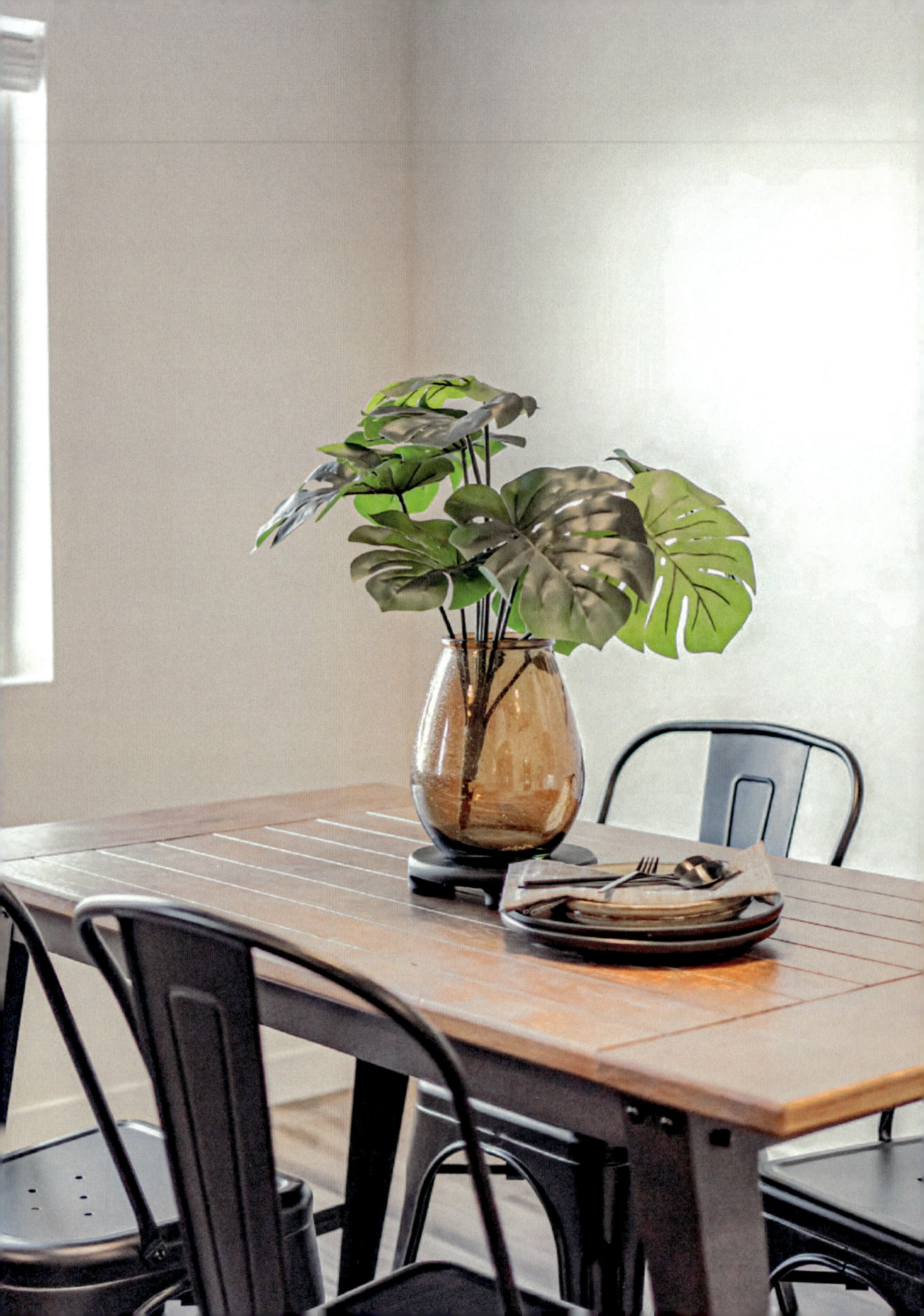

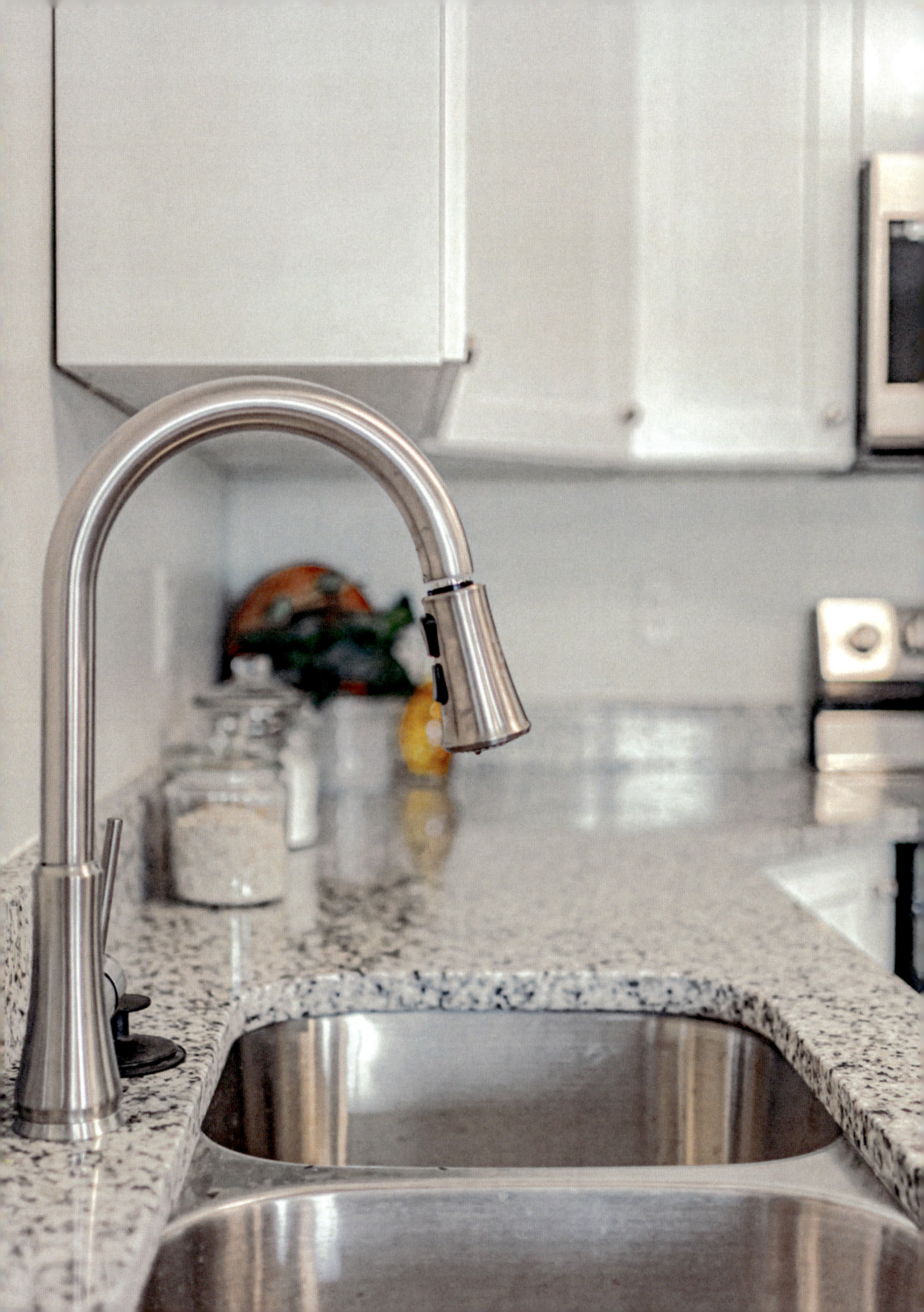

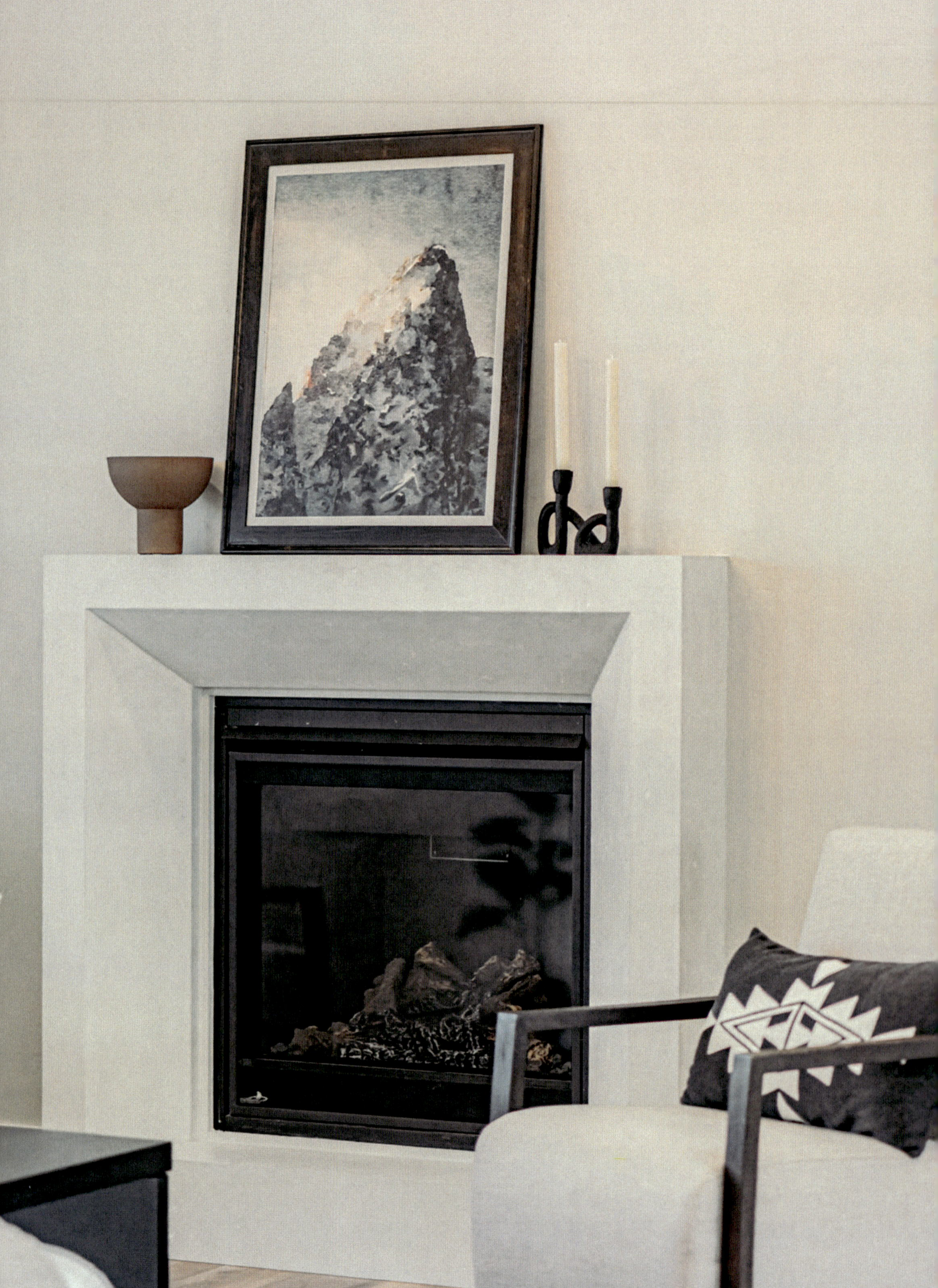

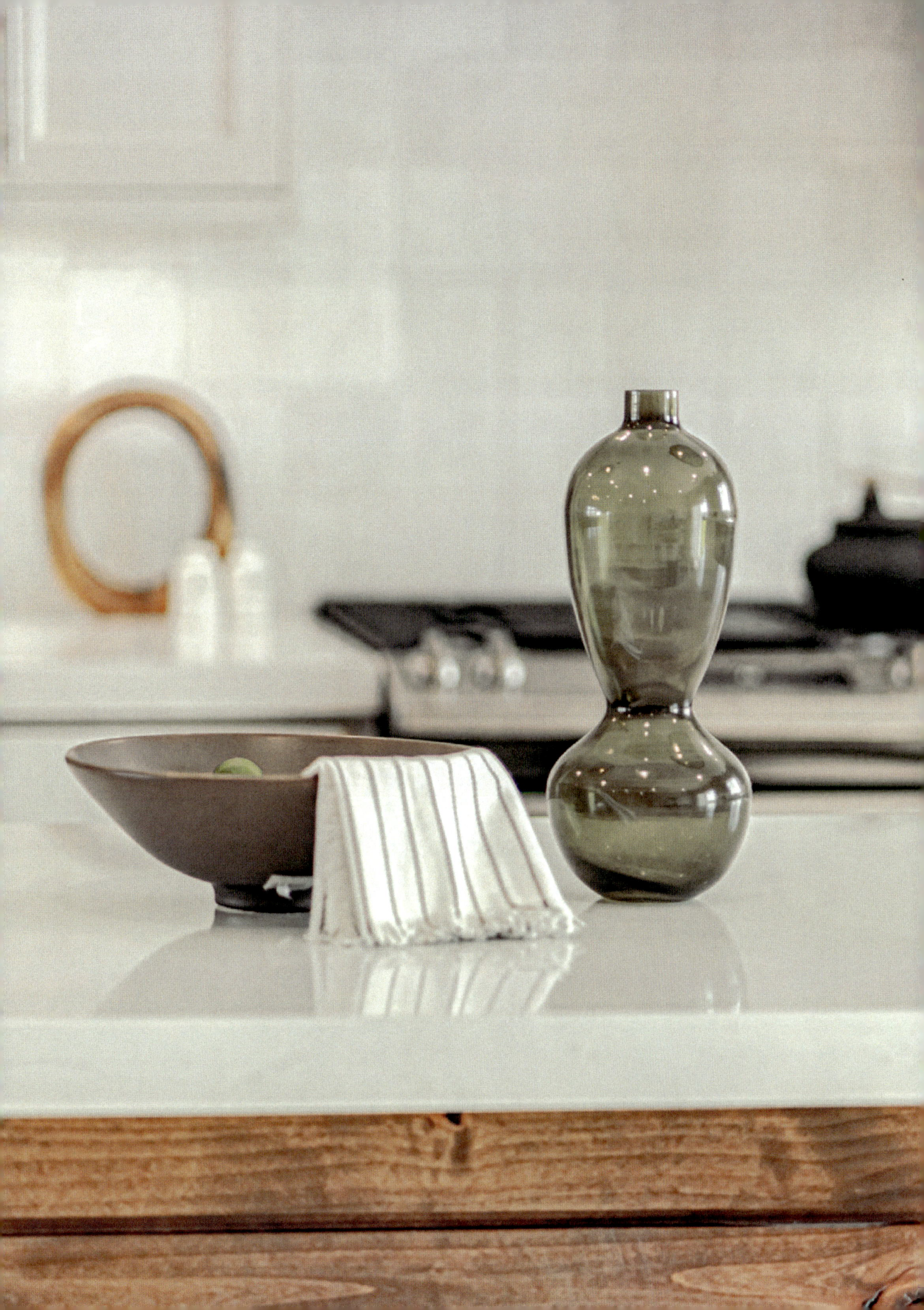

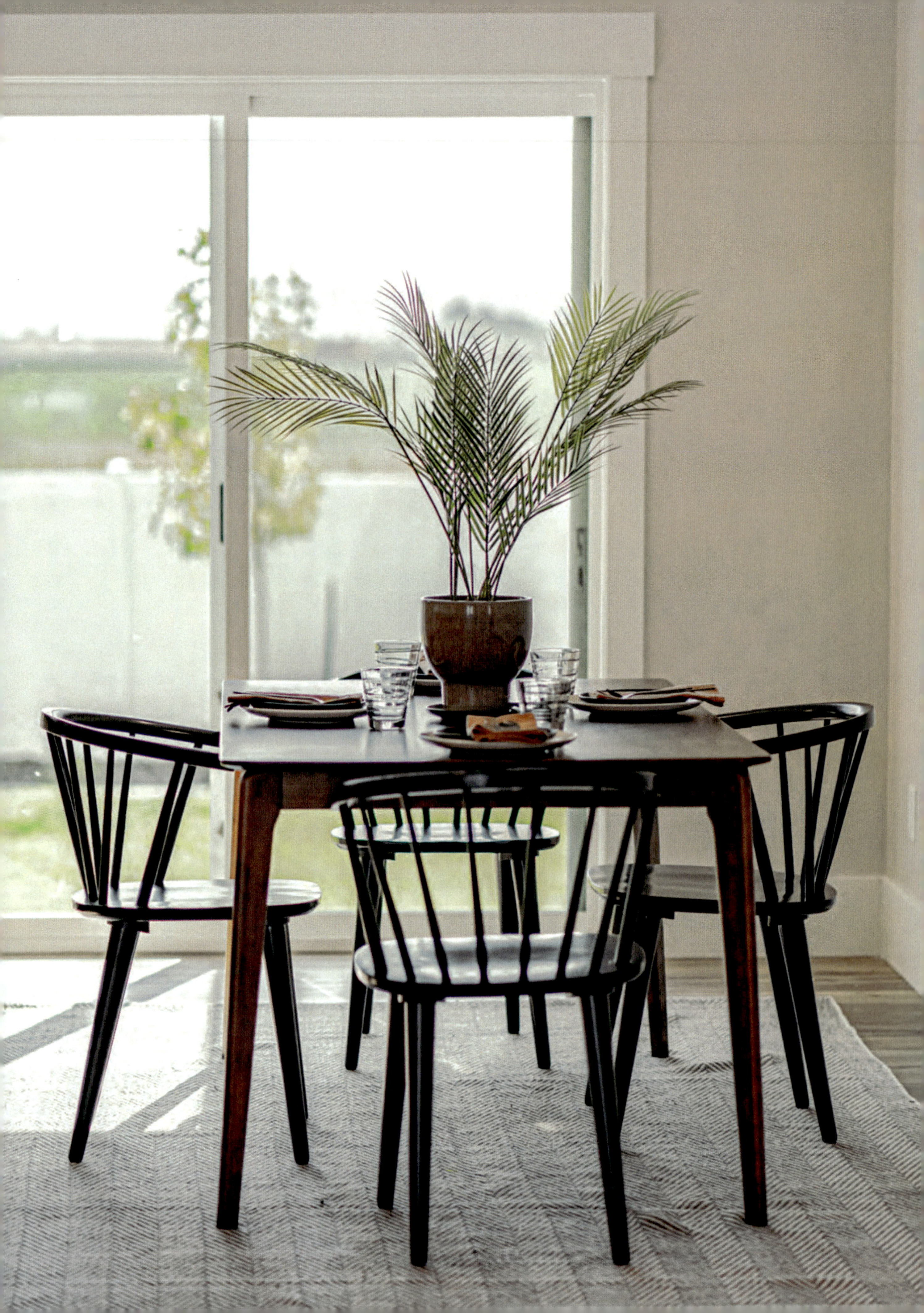

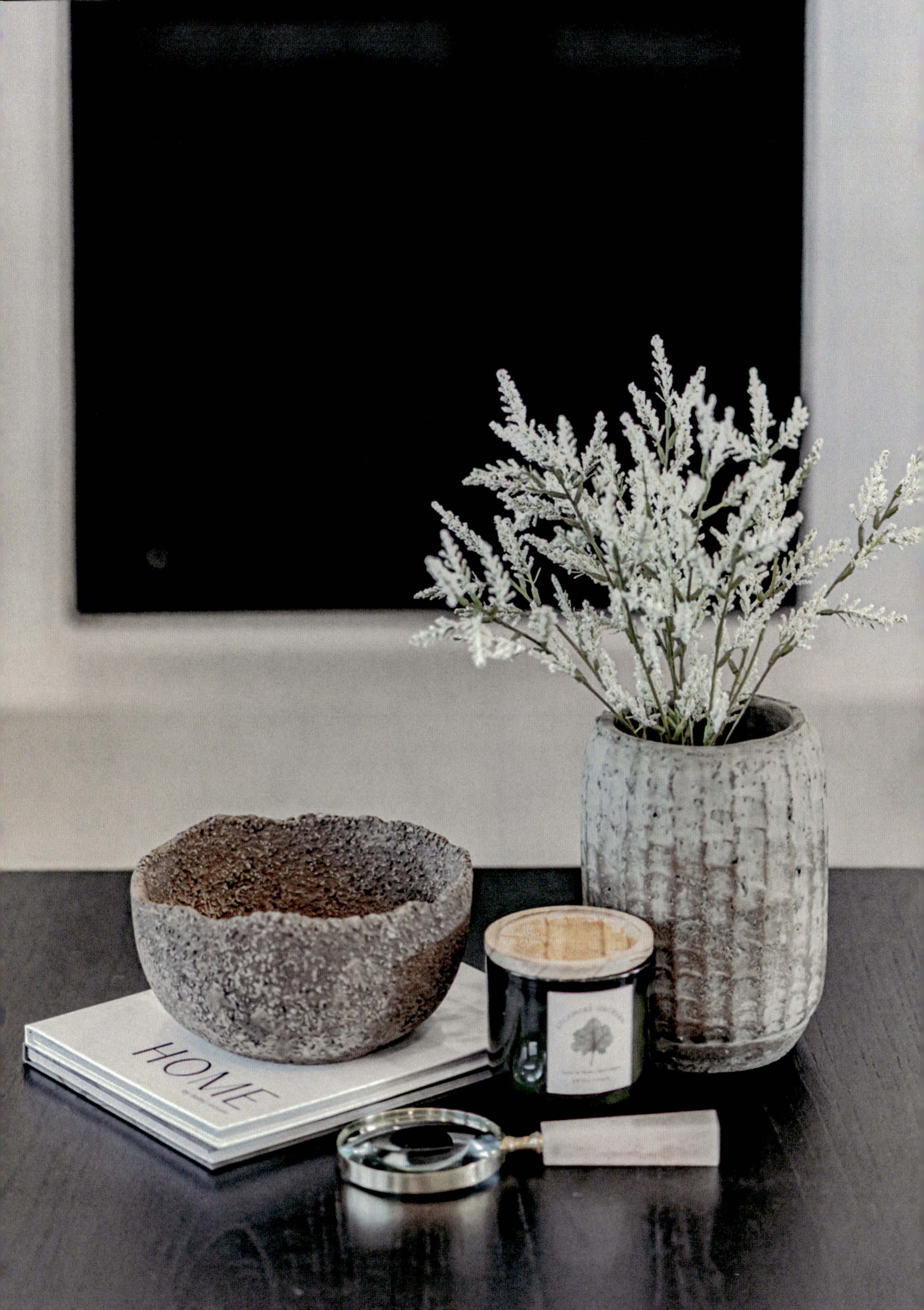
HOME

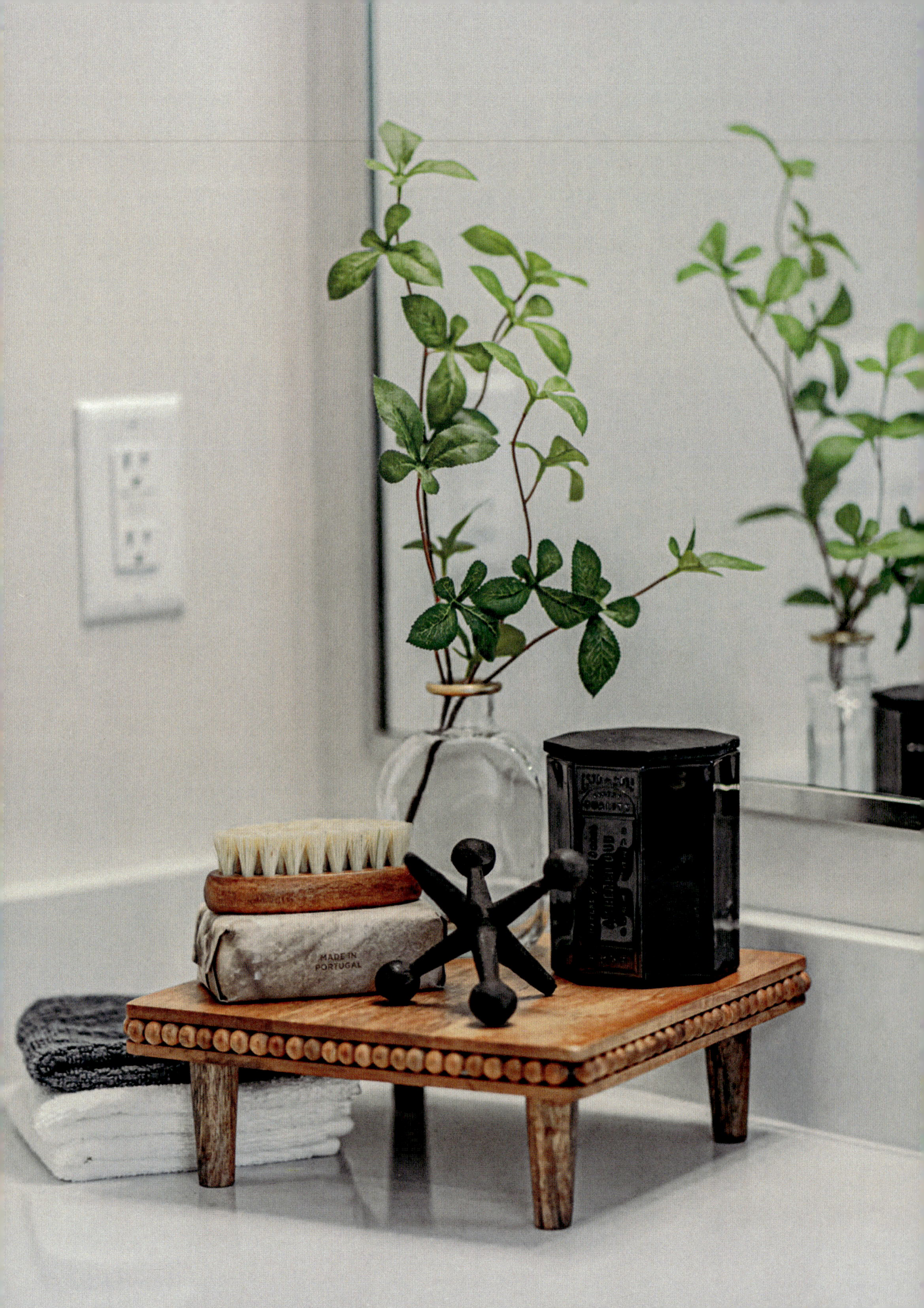
MADE IN
PORTUGAL

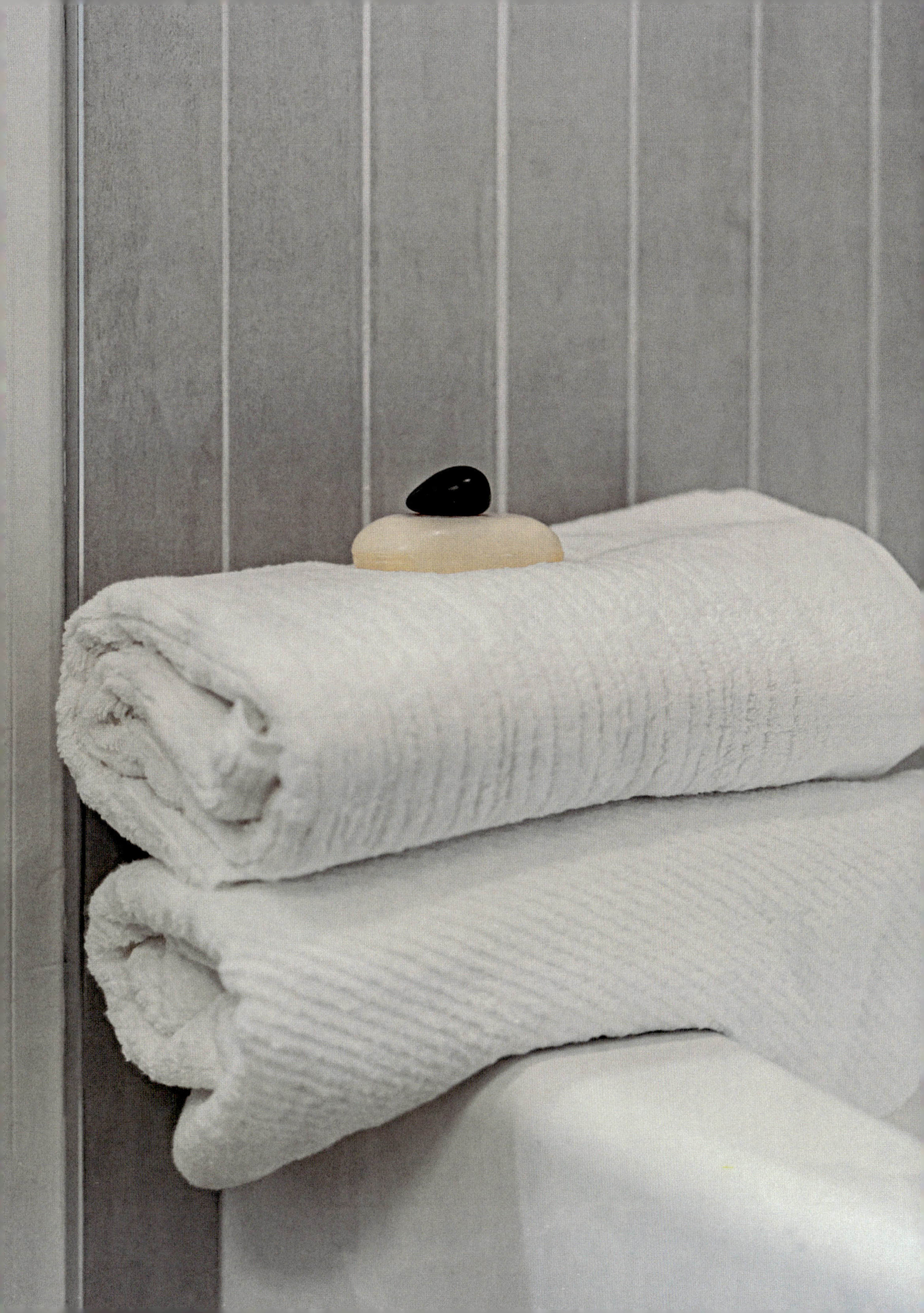

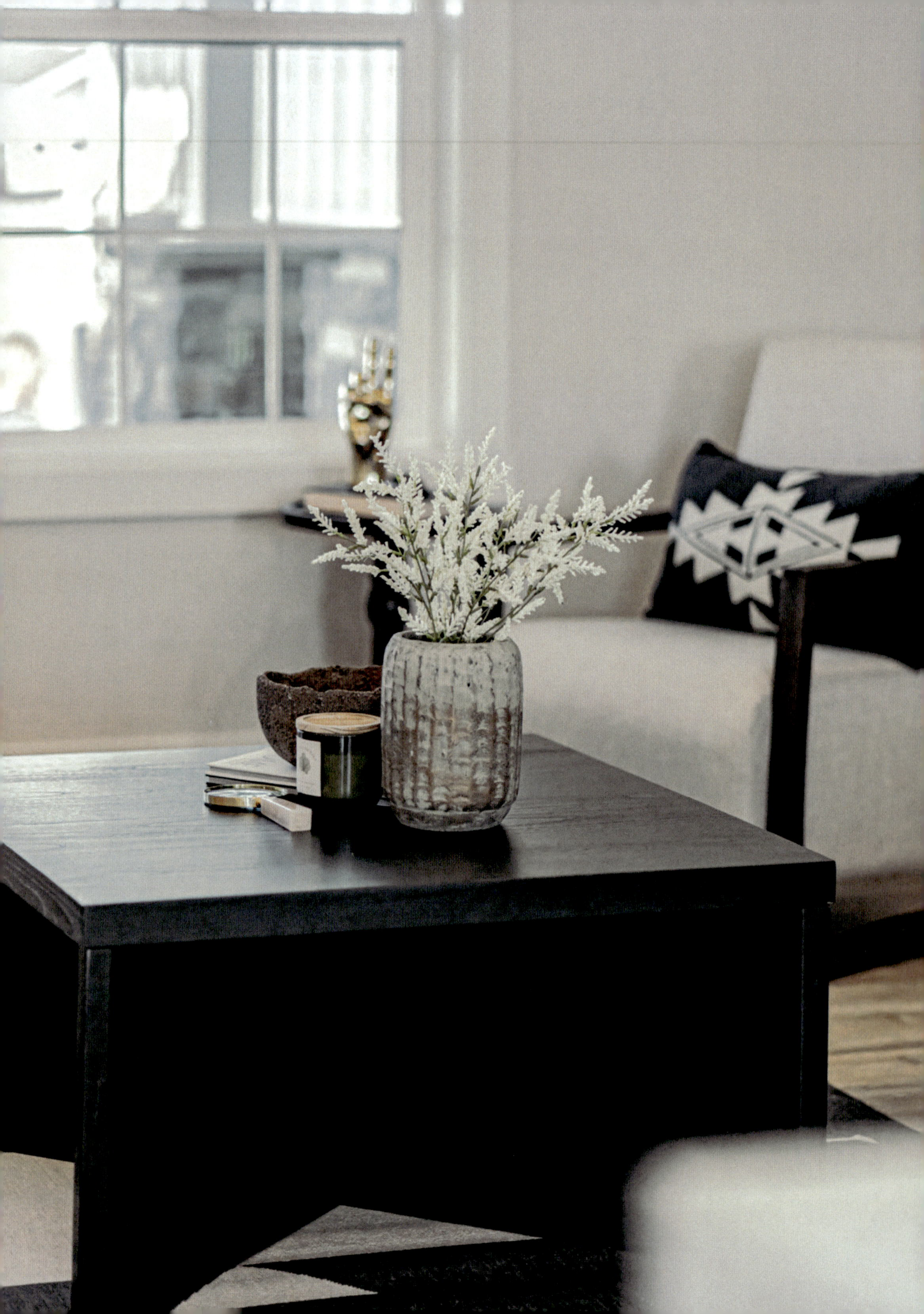

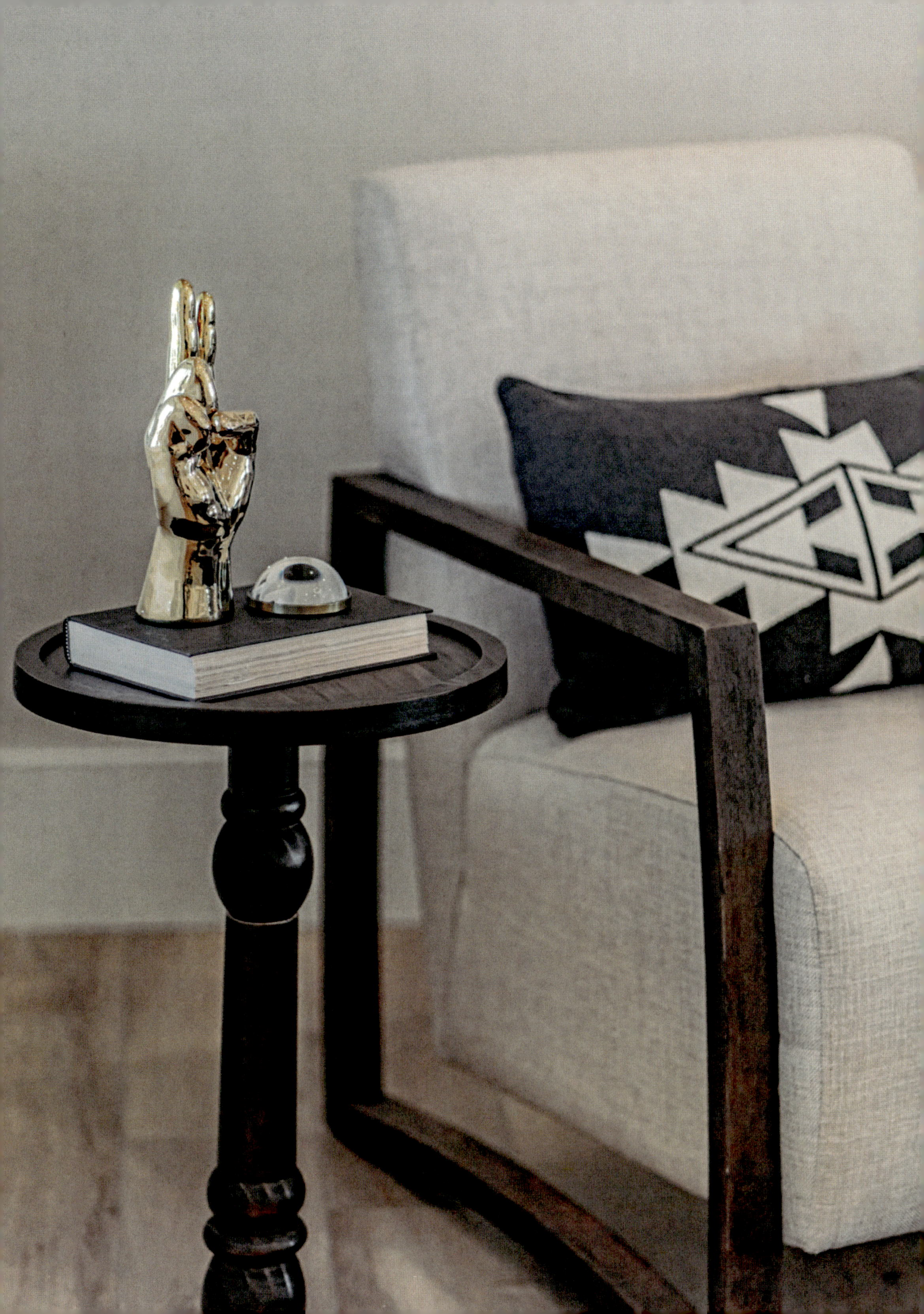

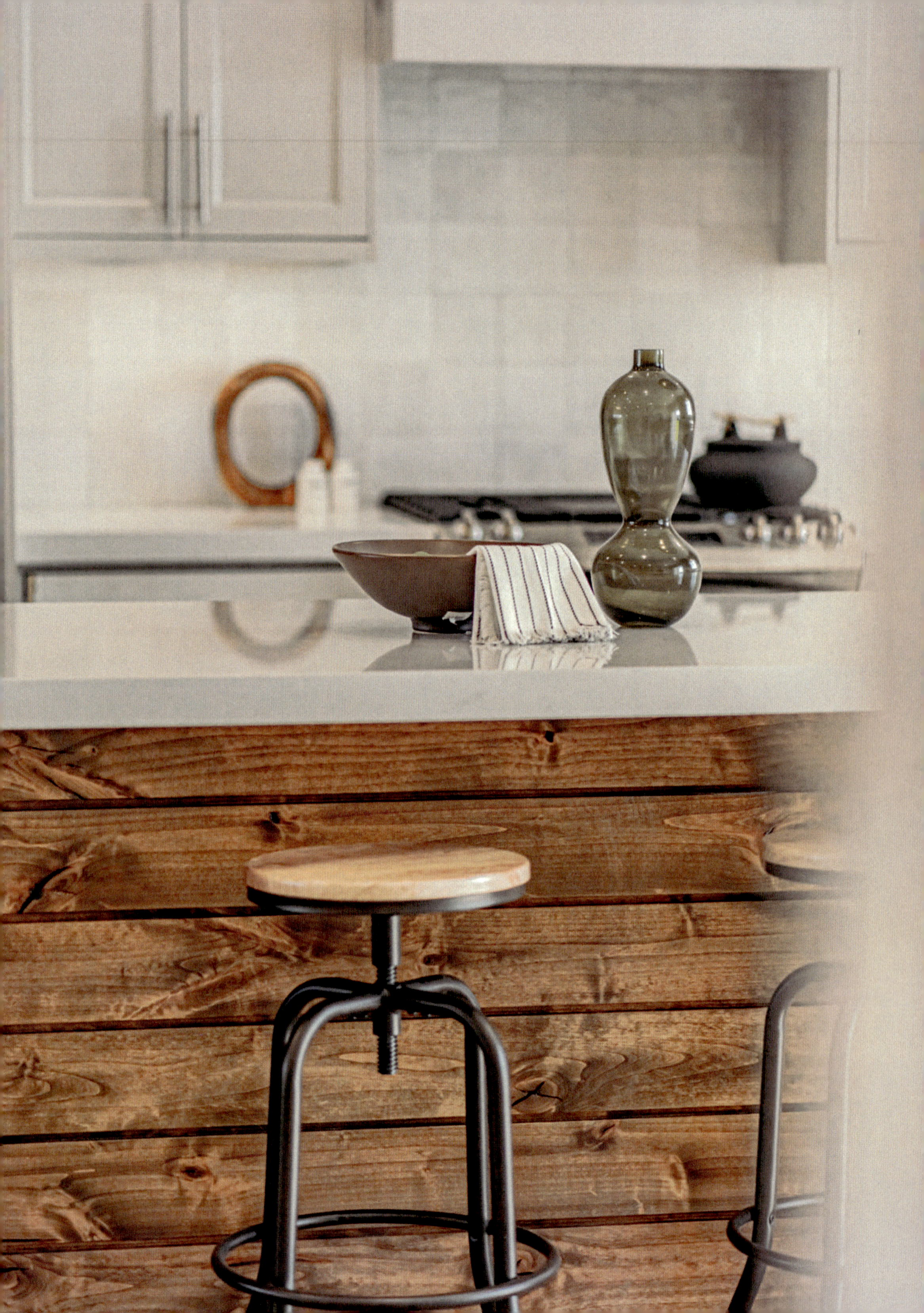

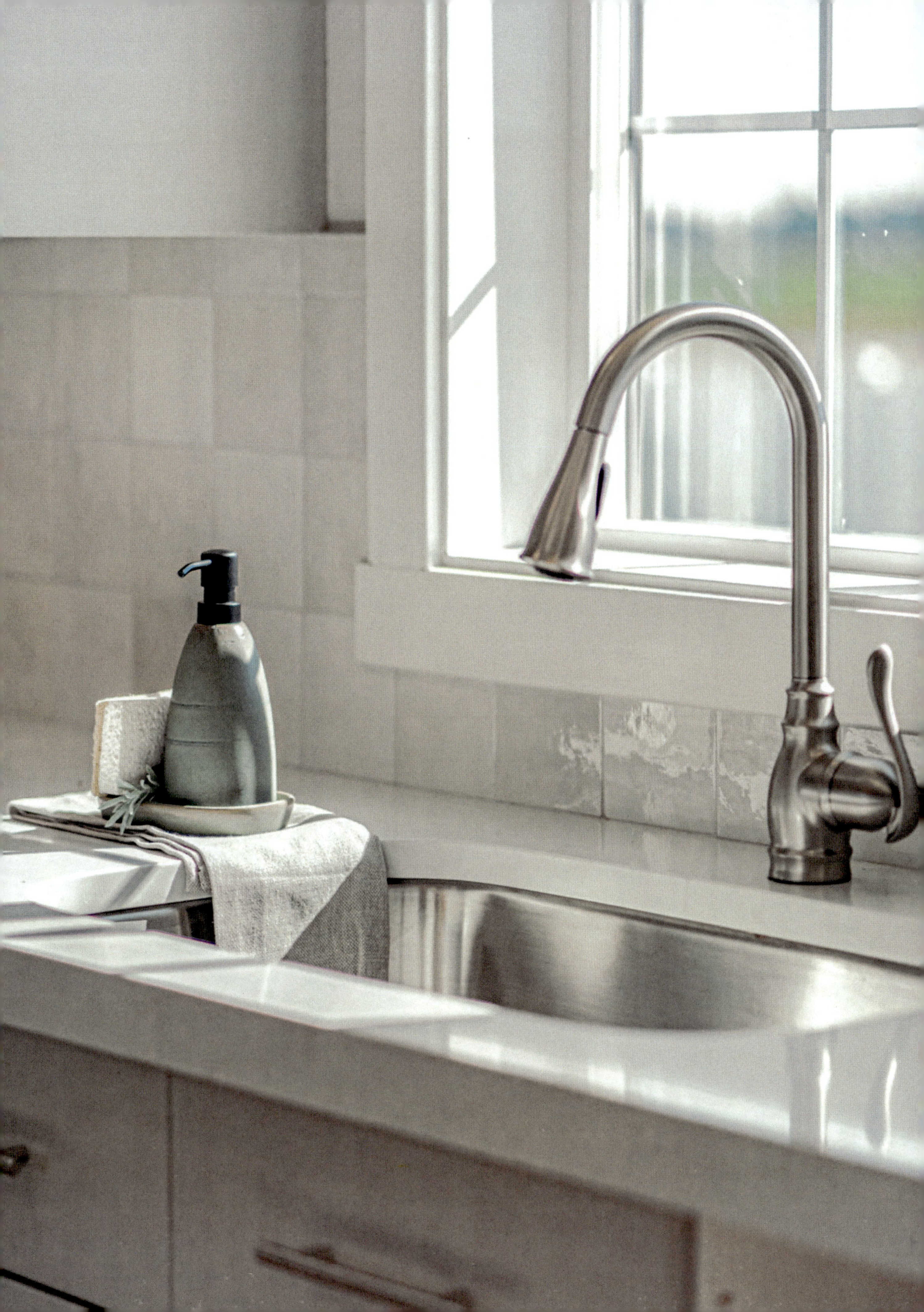

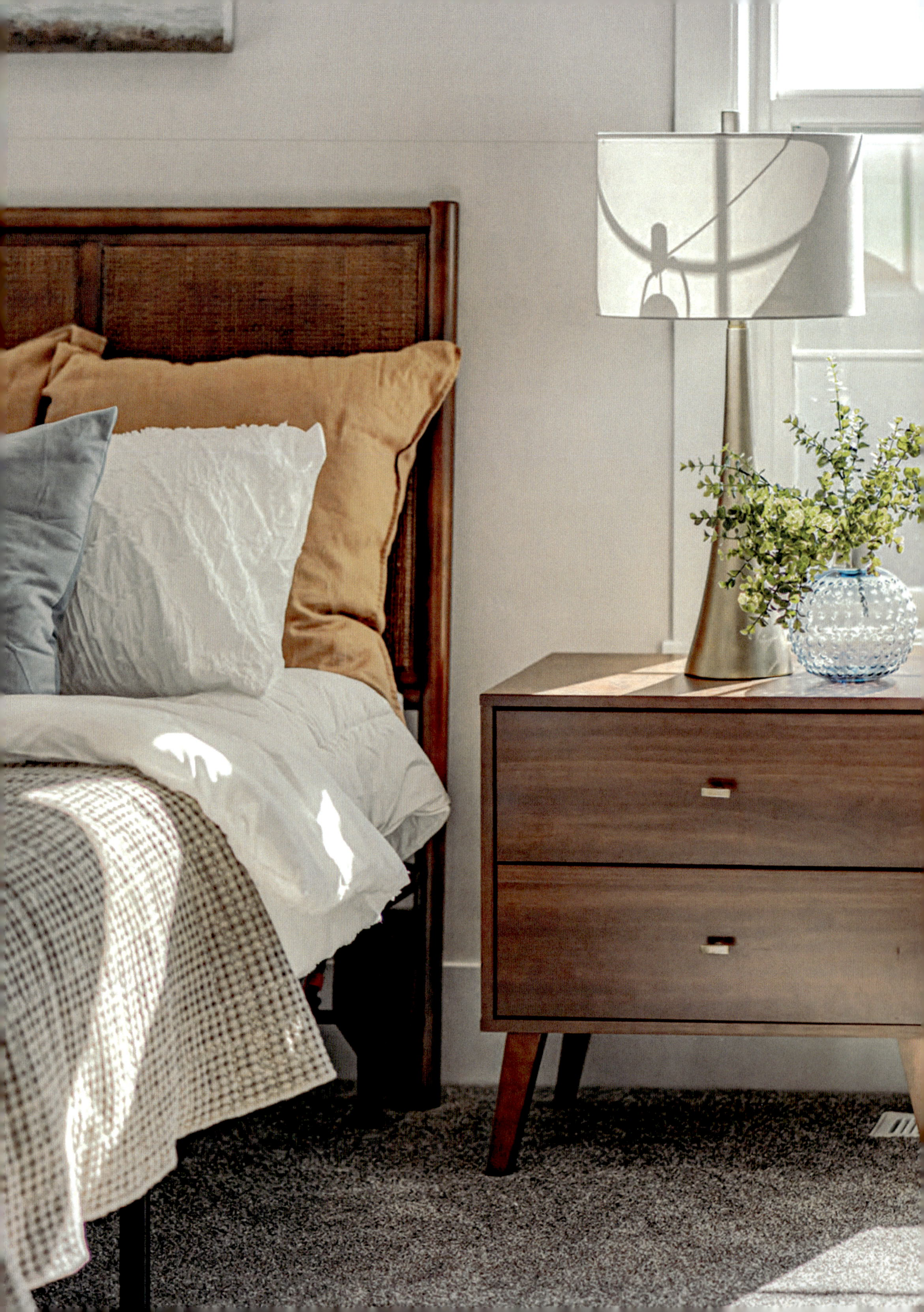

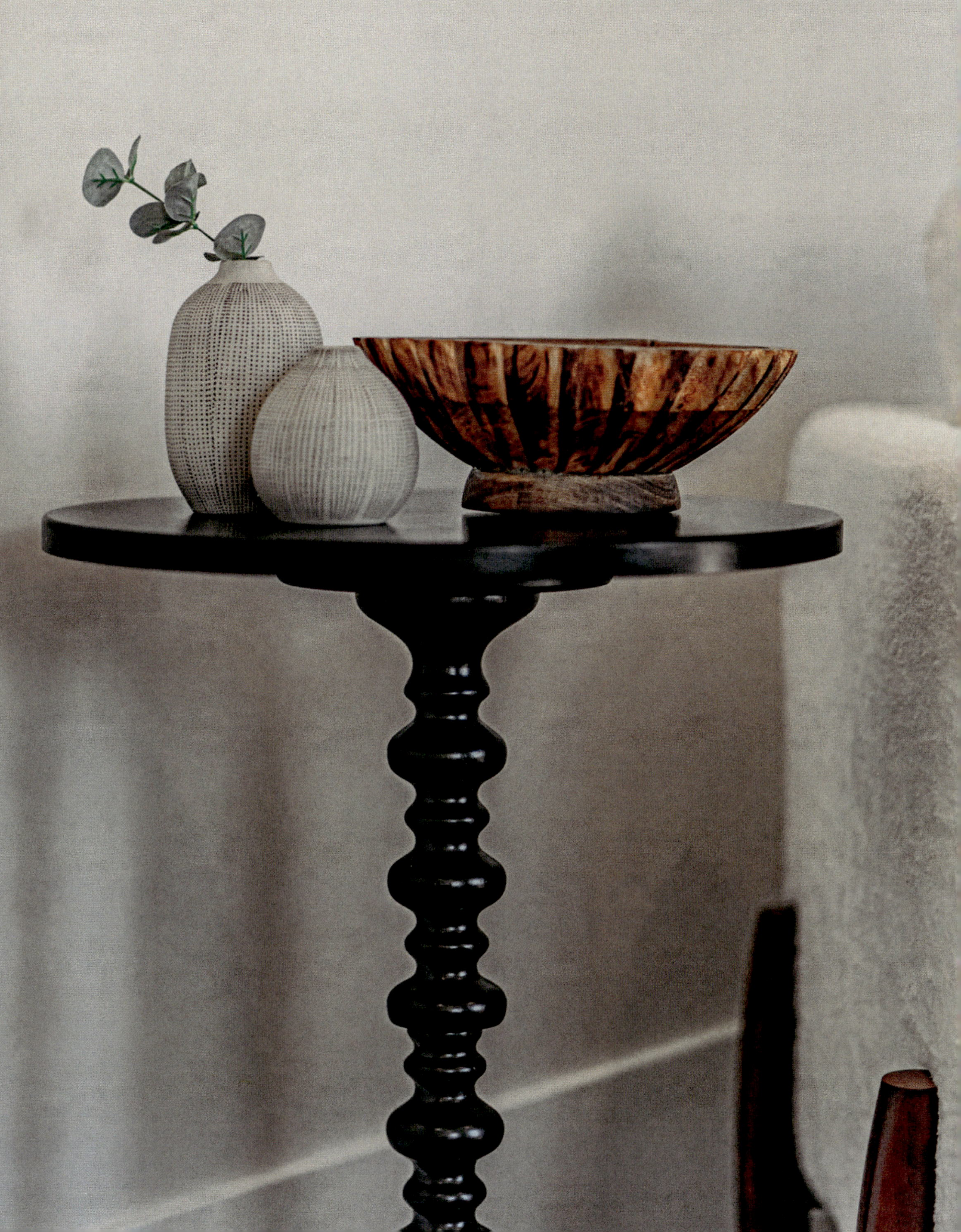

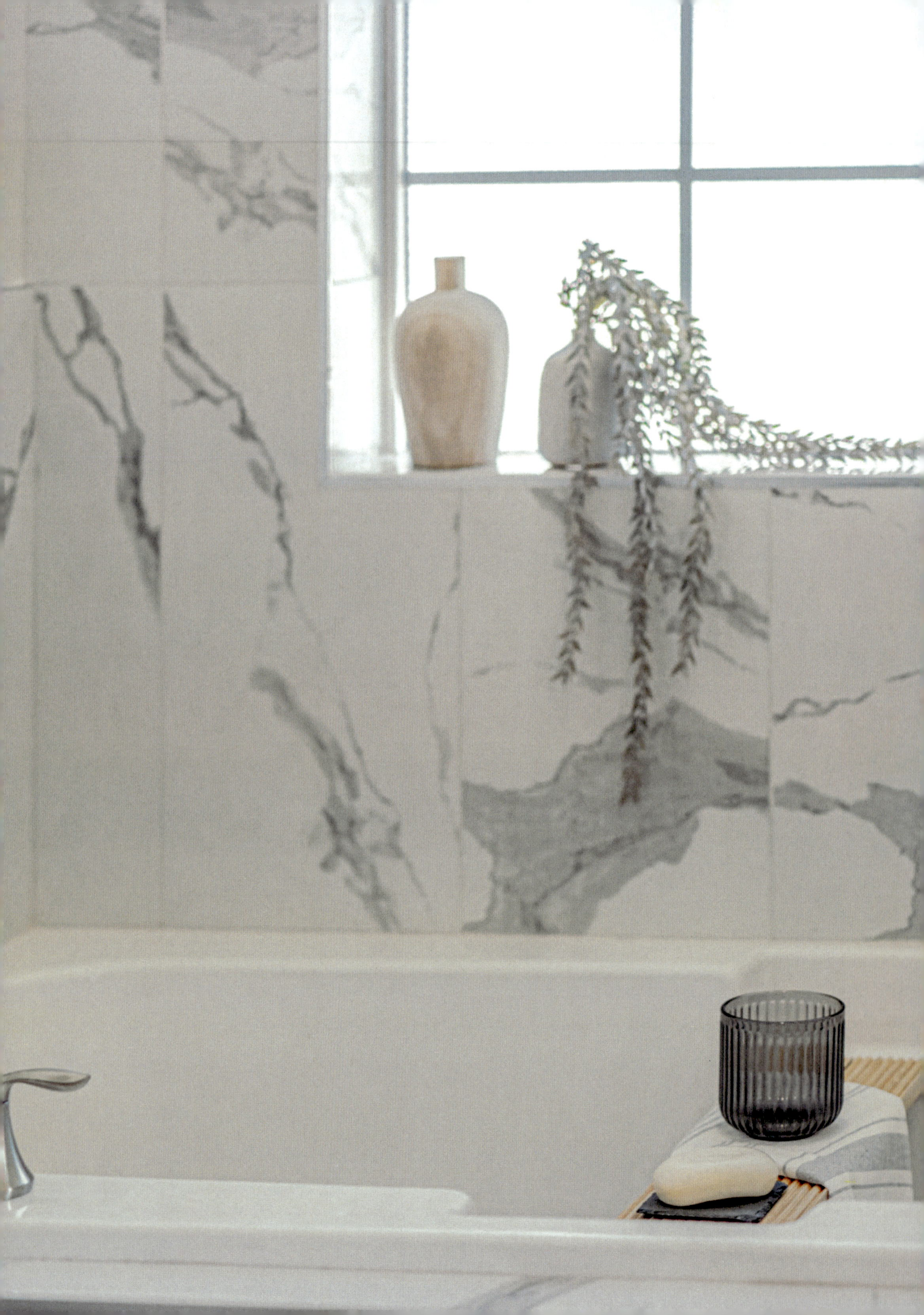

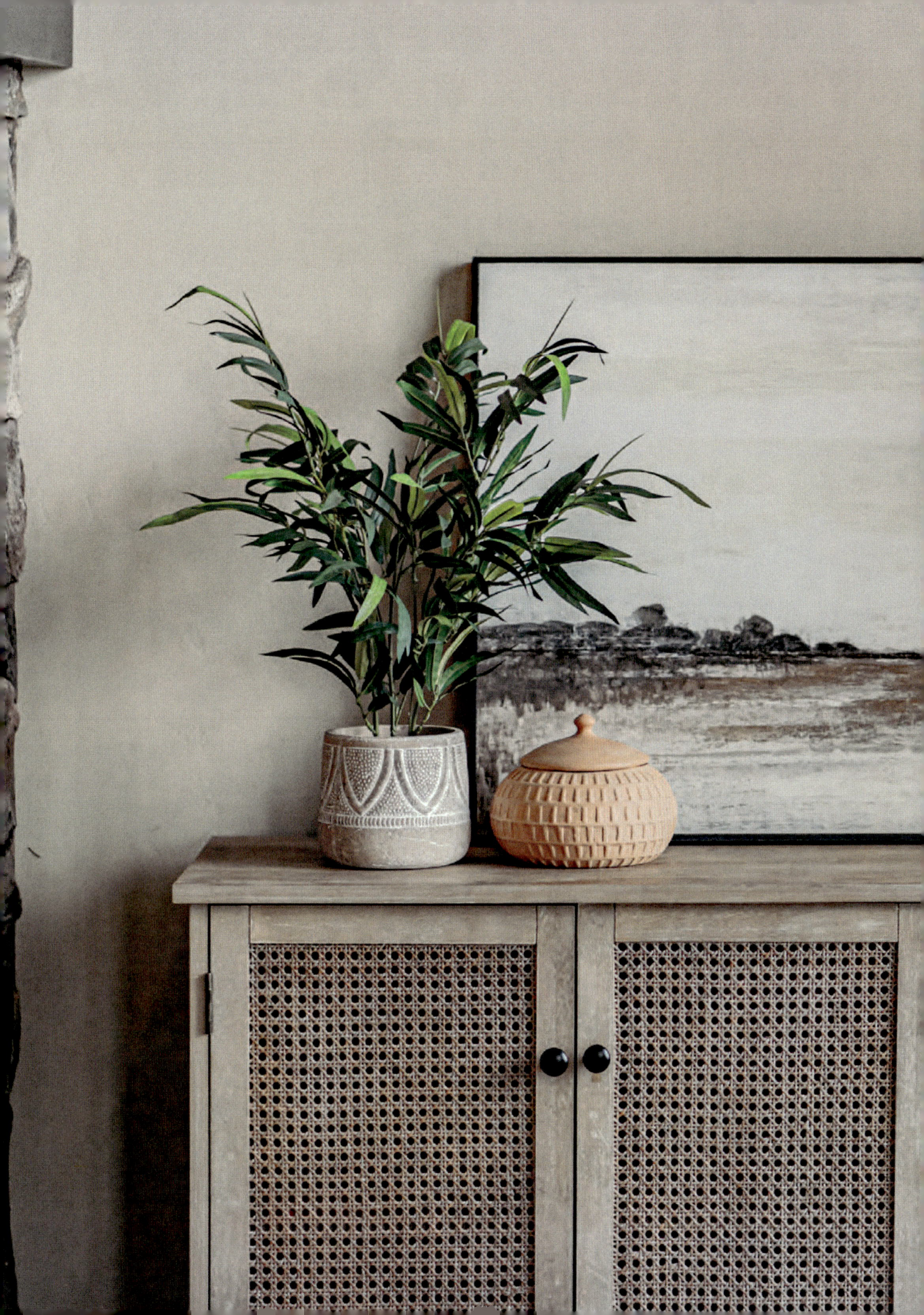

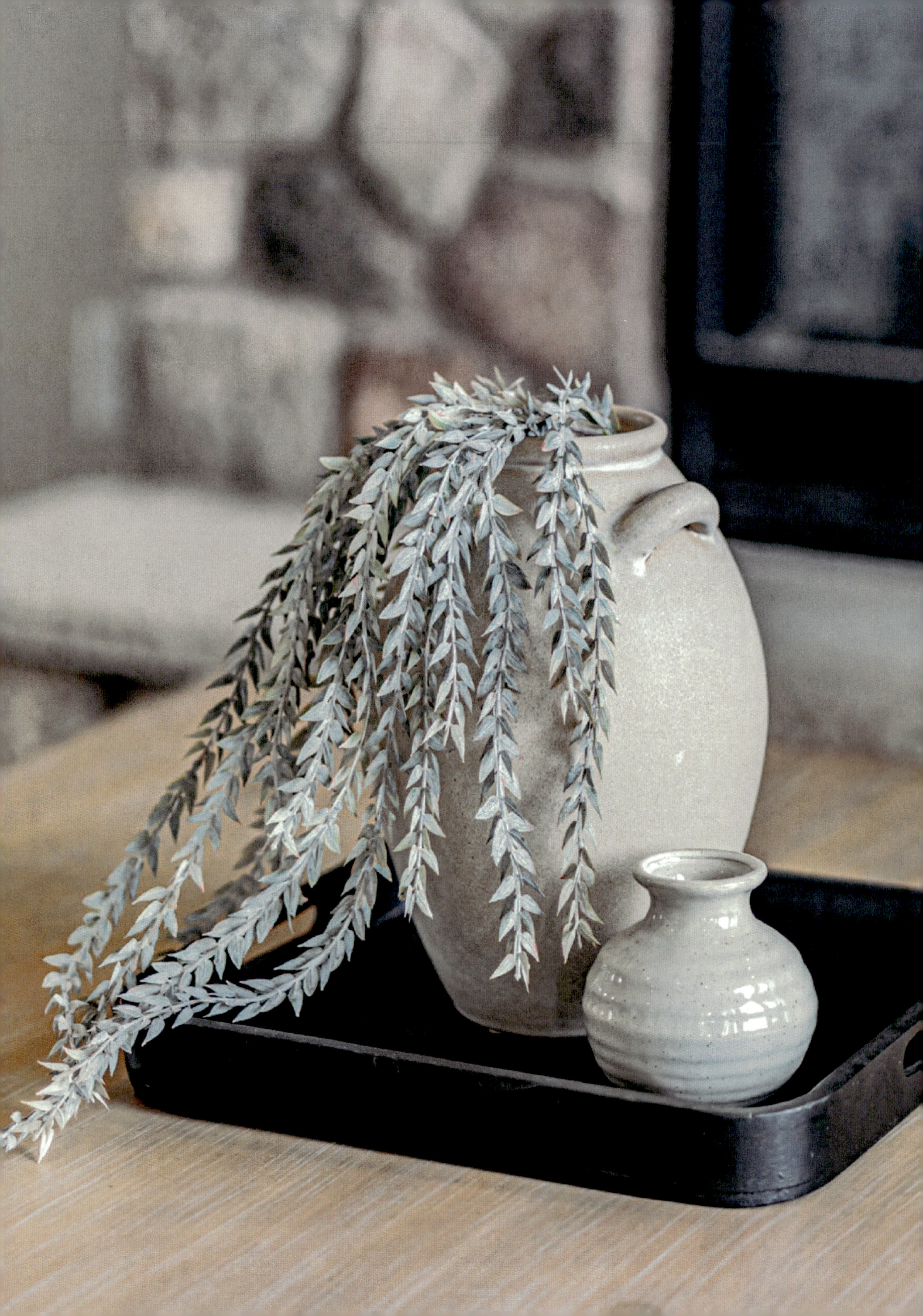

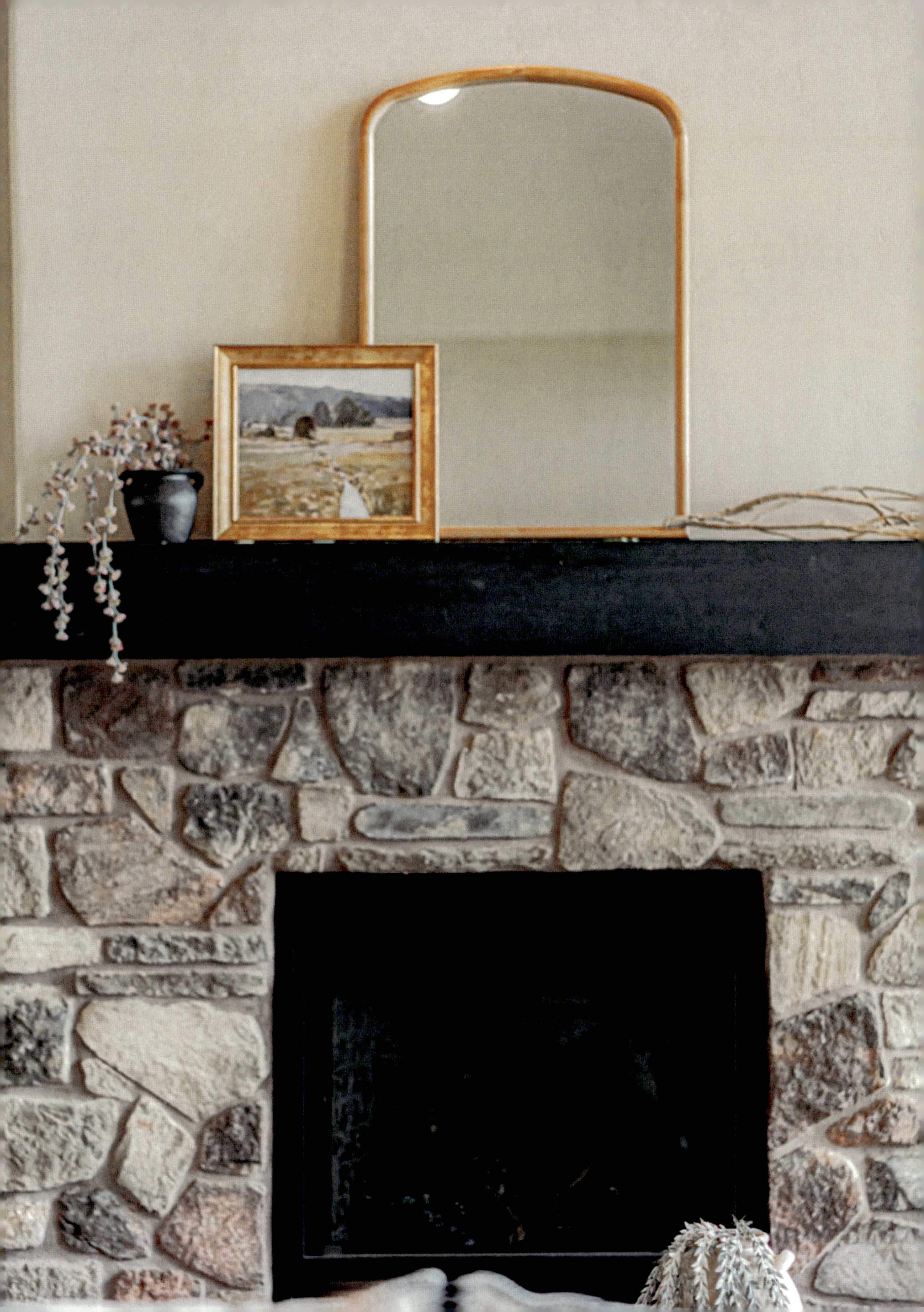

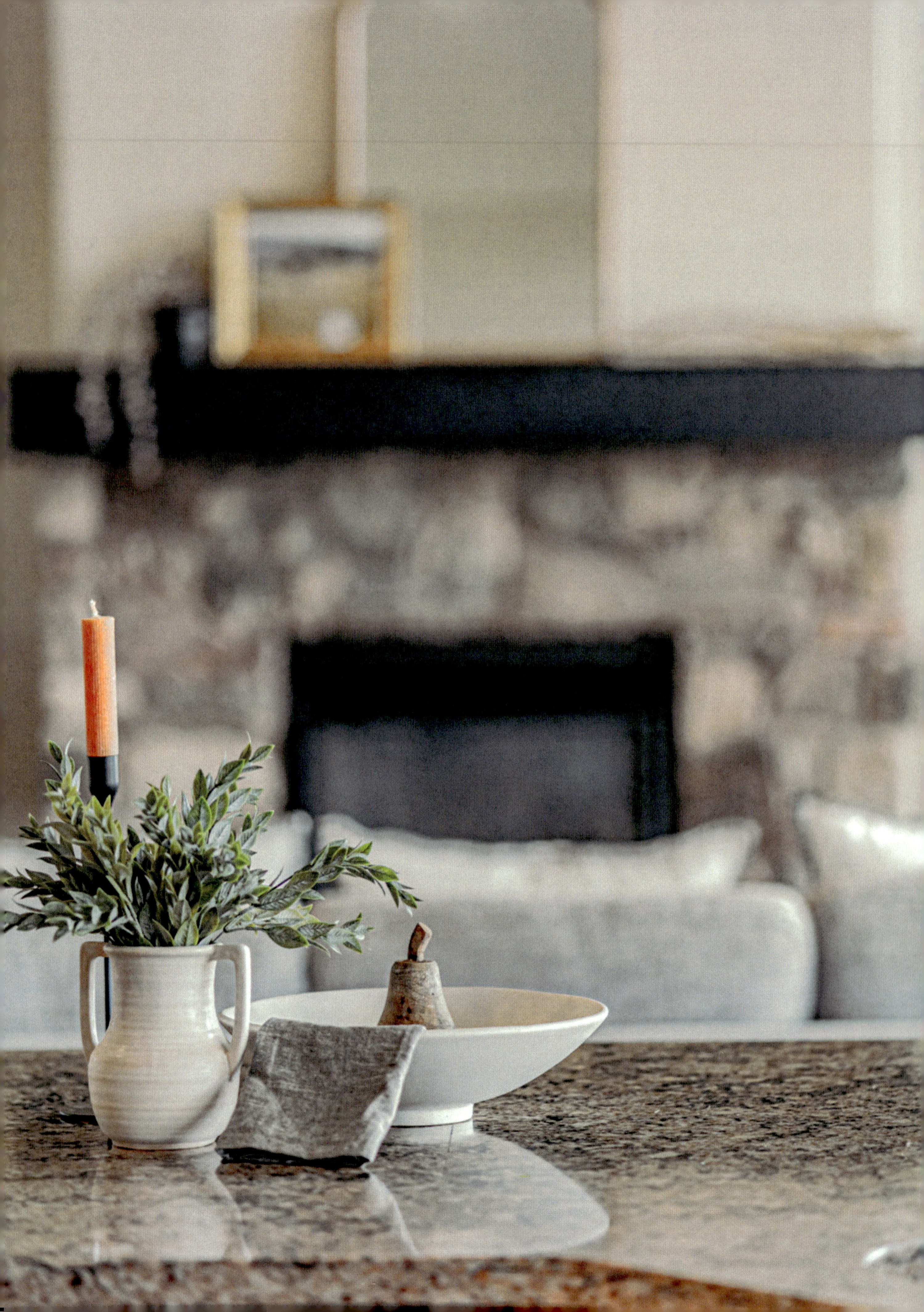

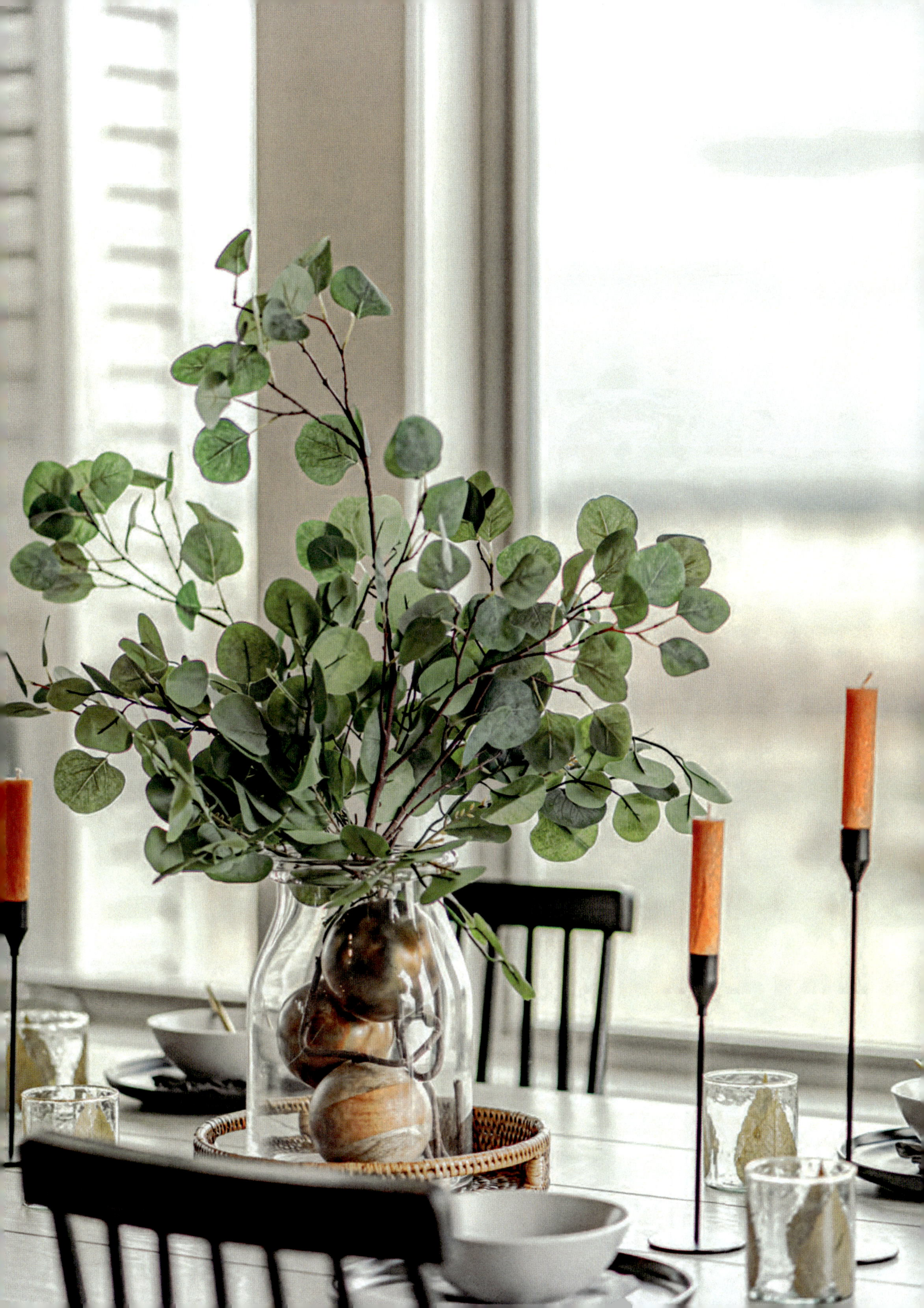

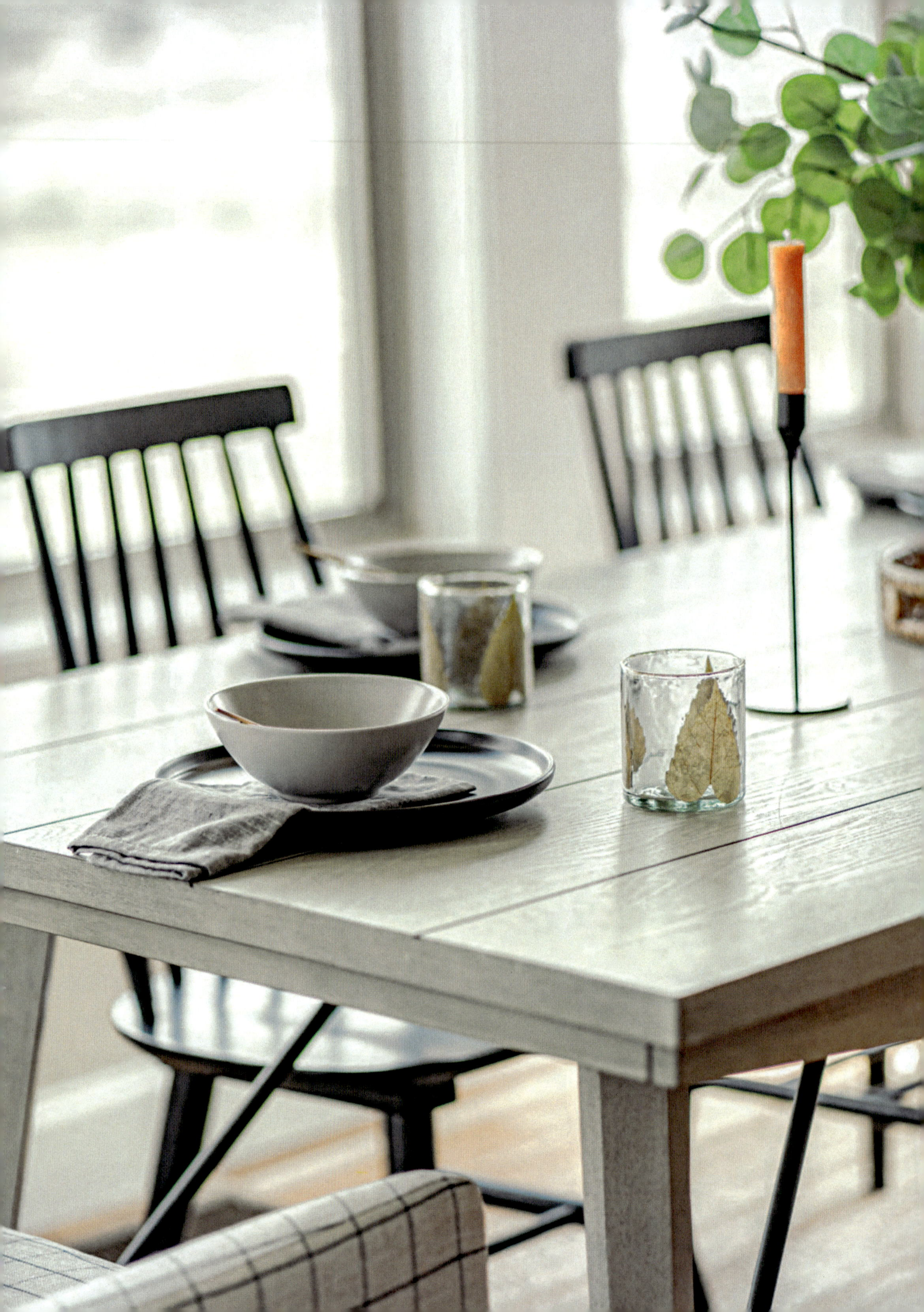

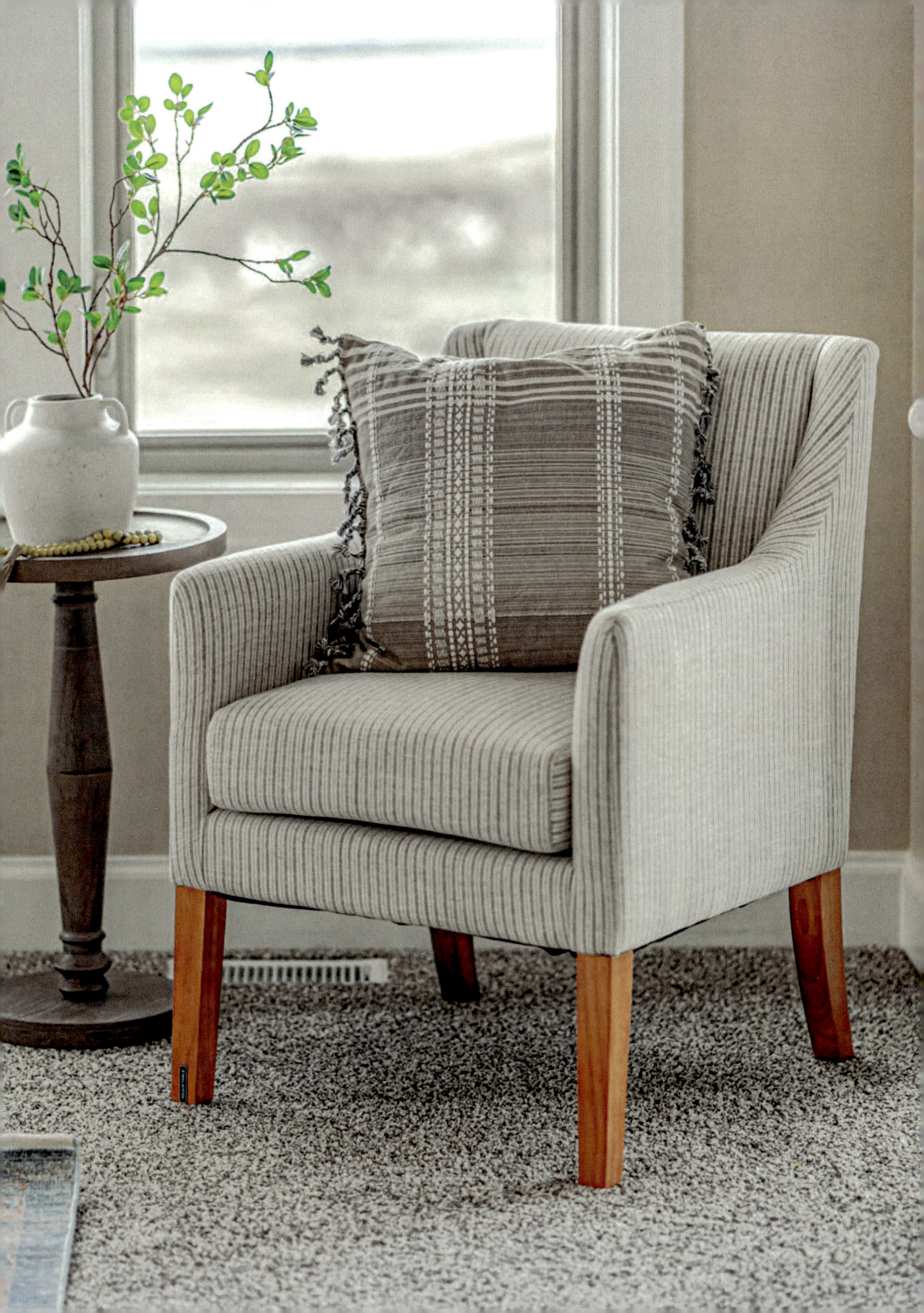

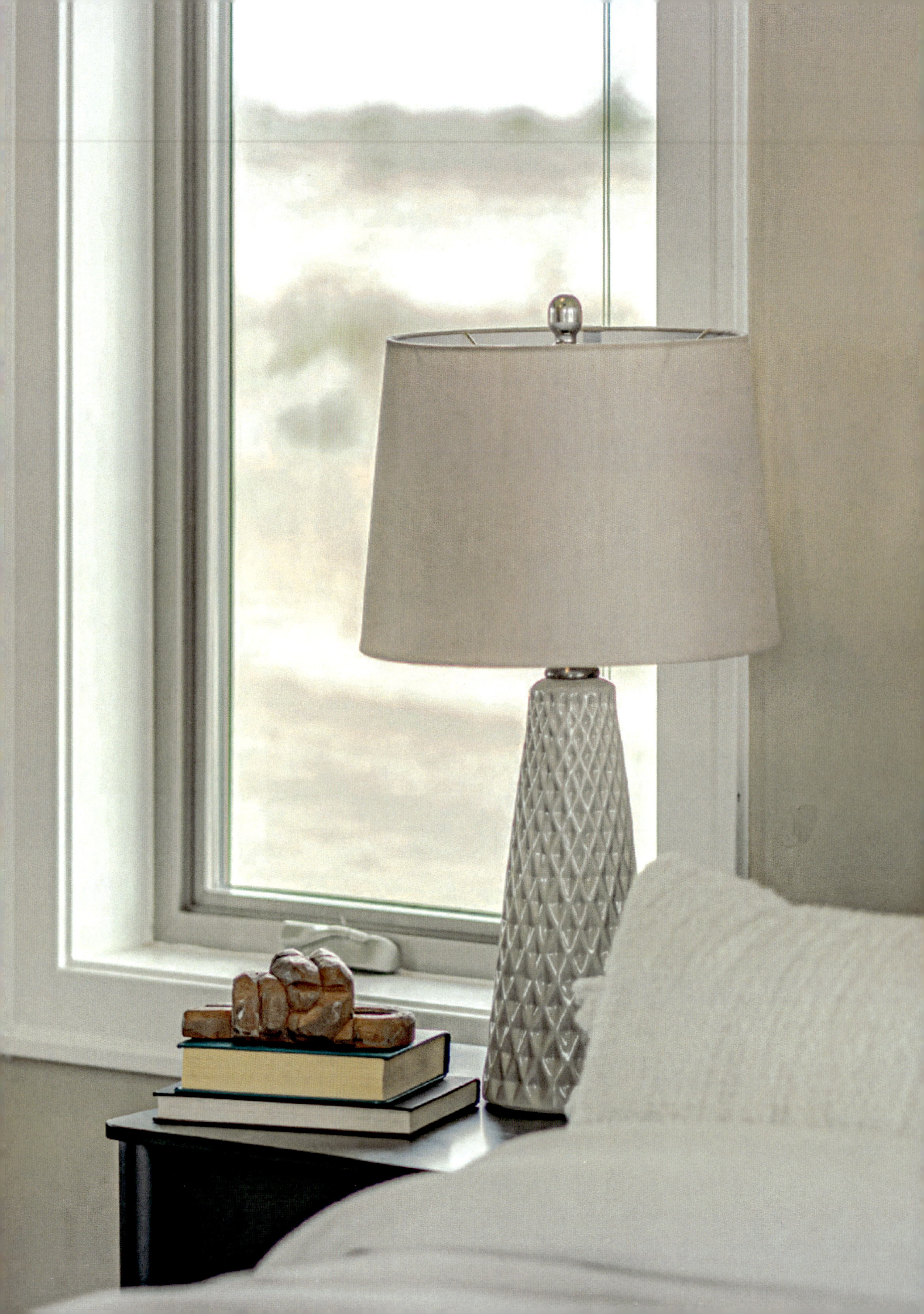

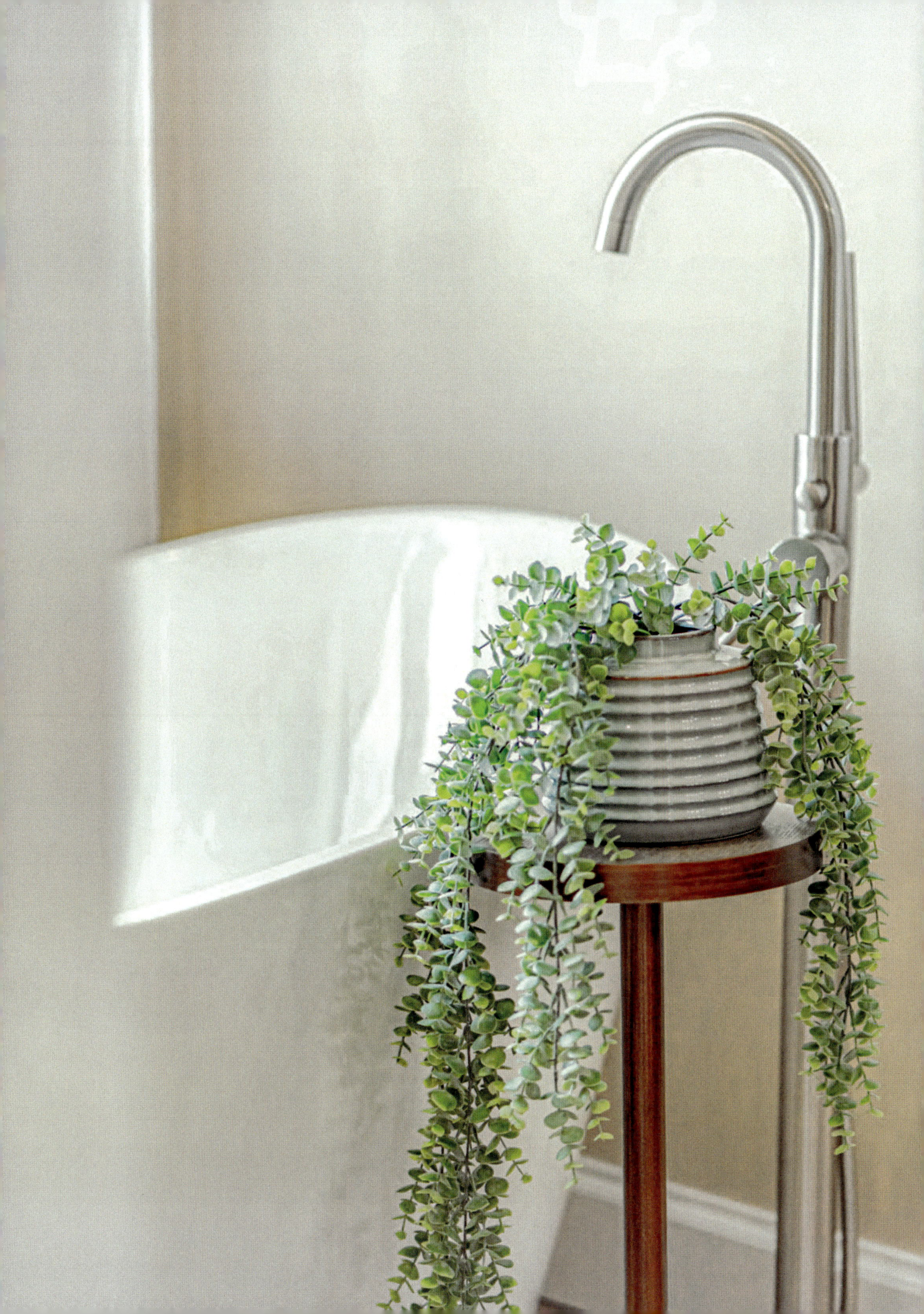

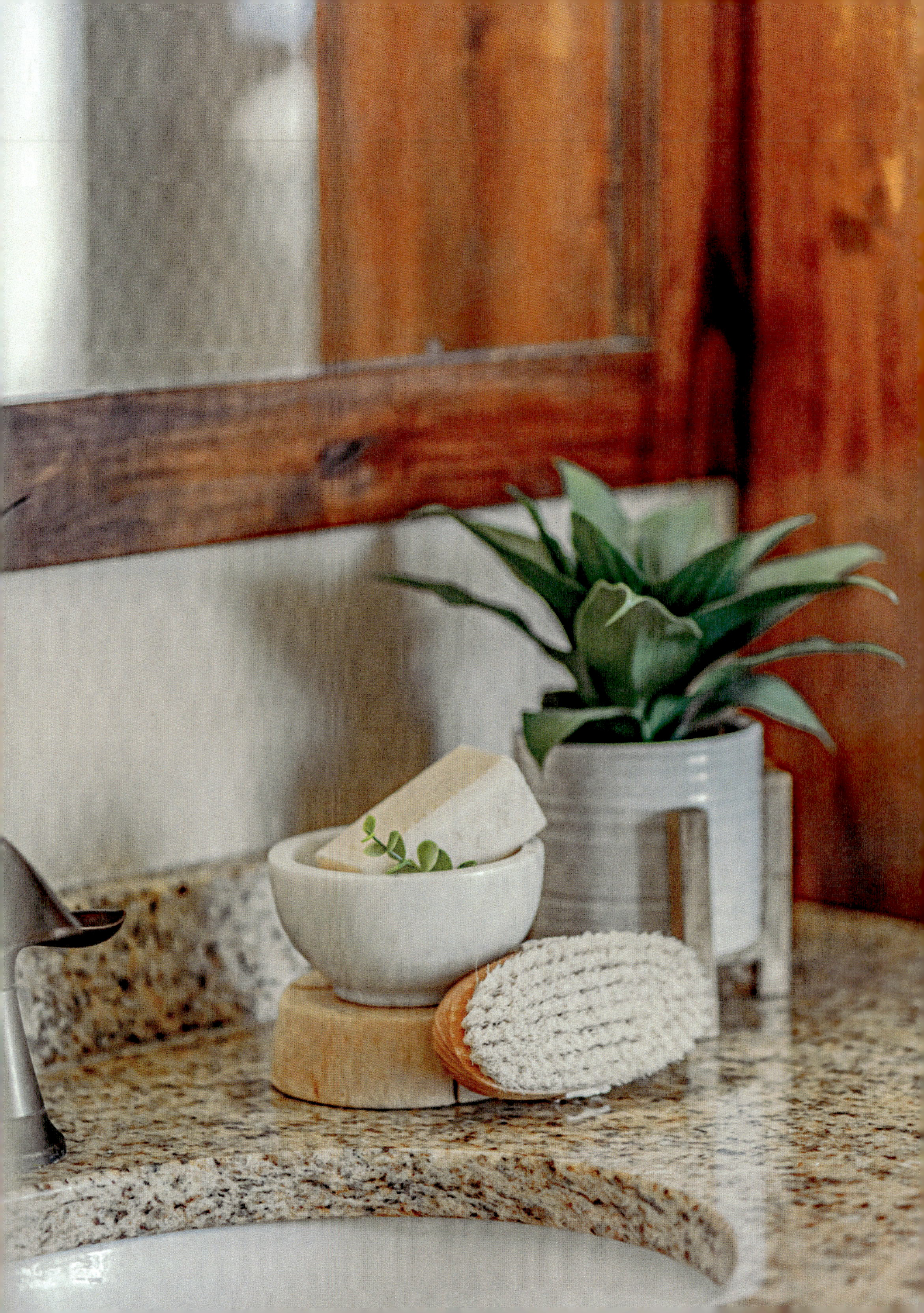

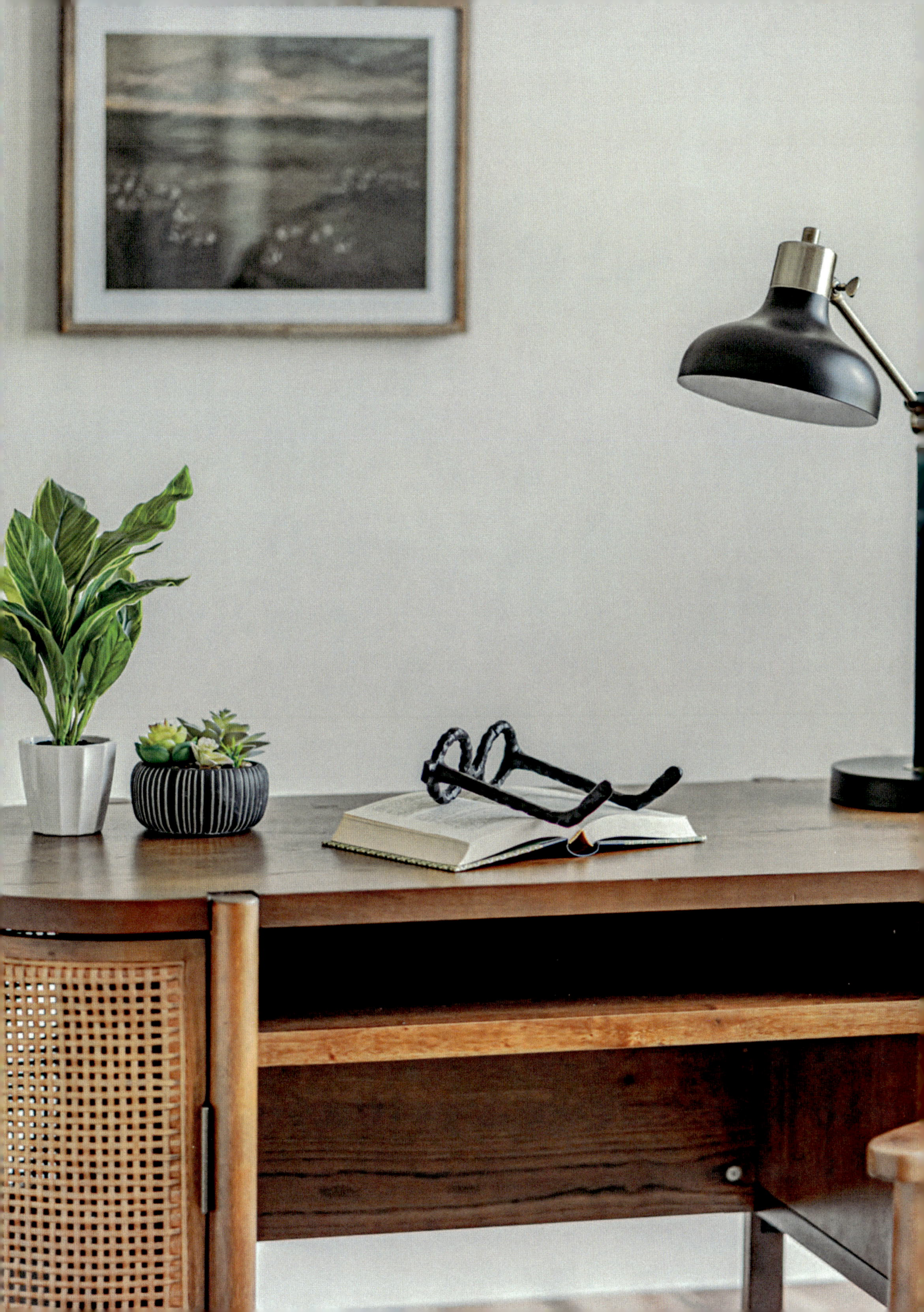

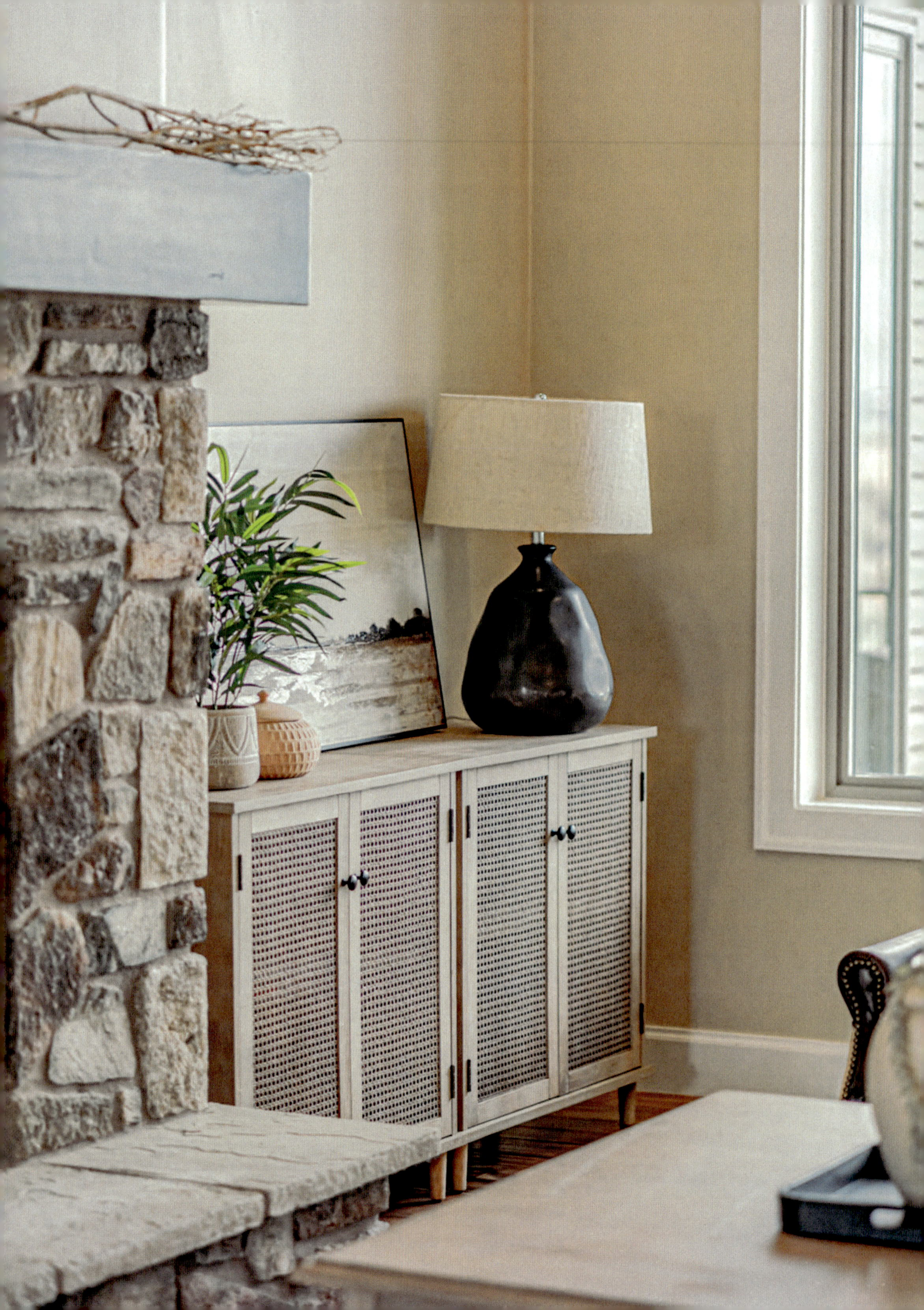

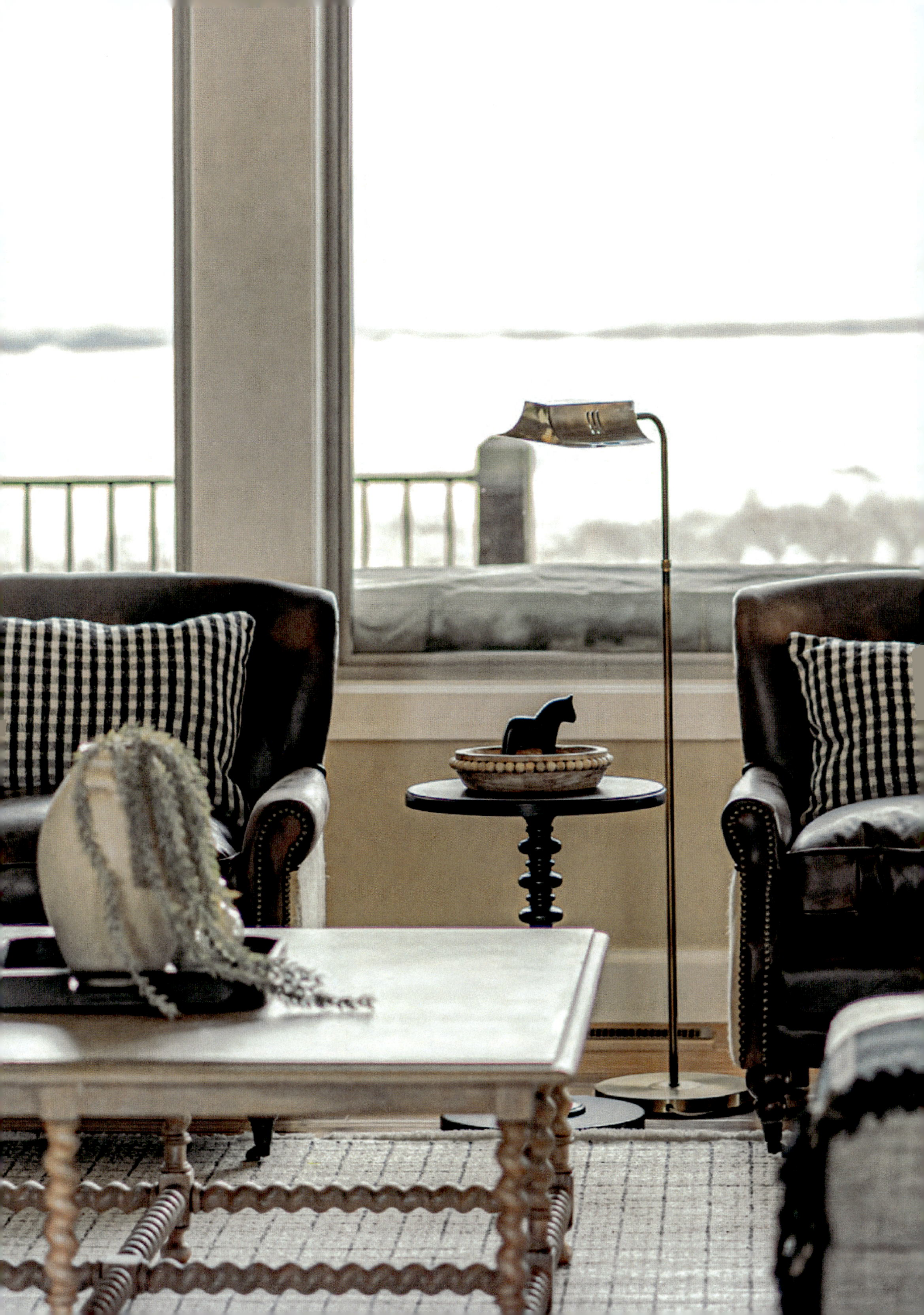

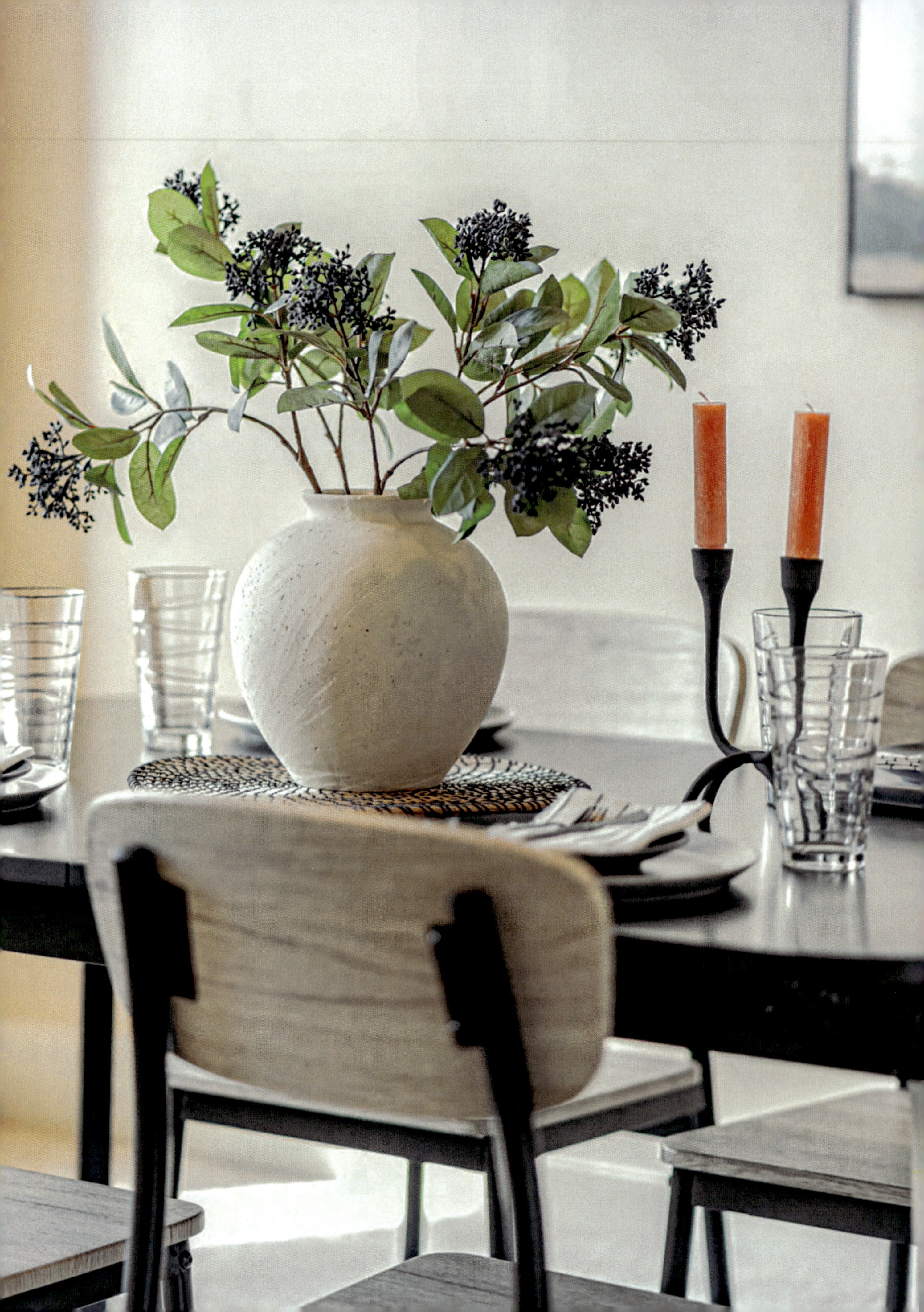

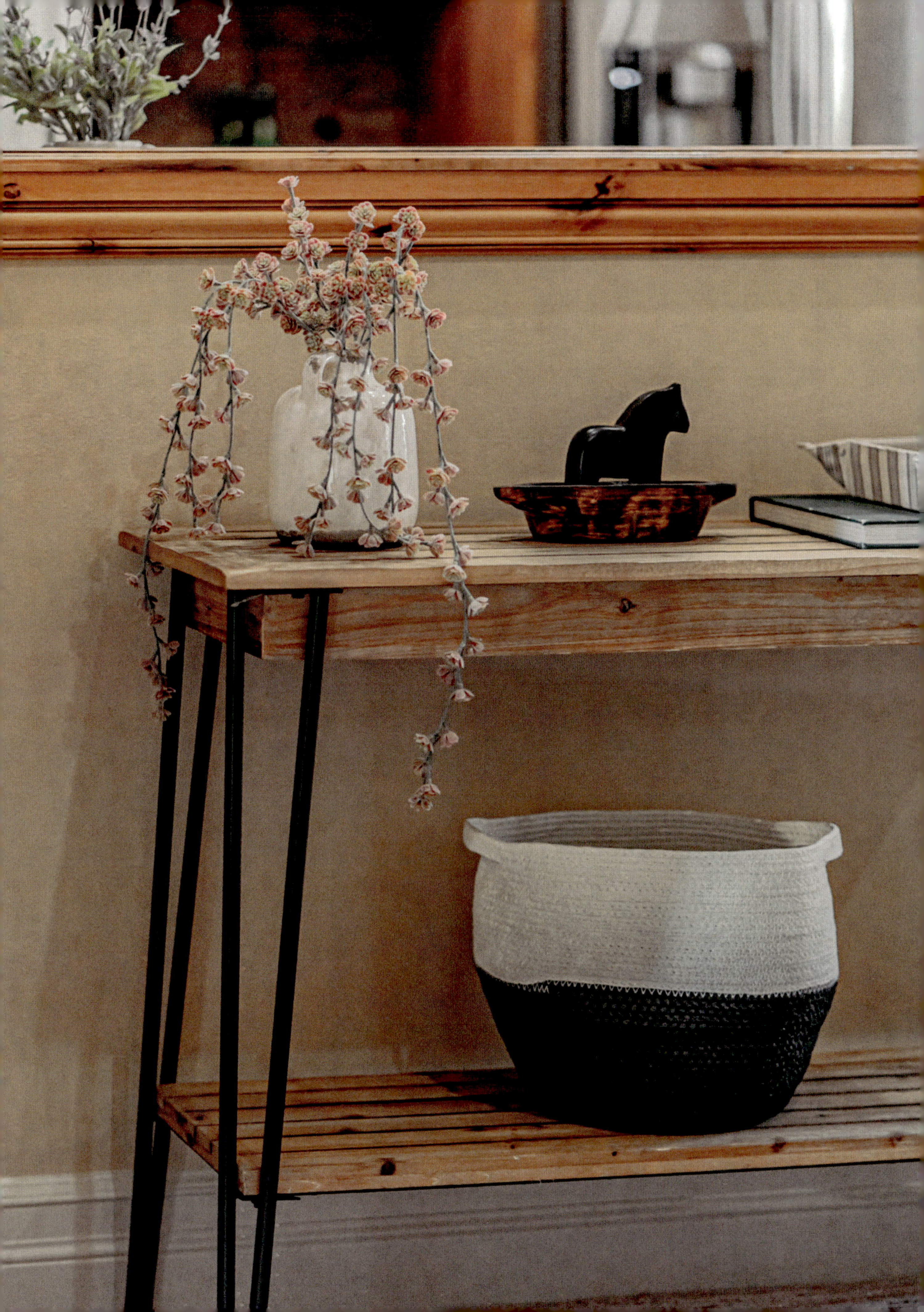

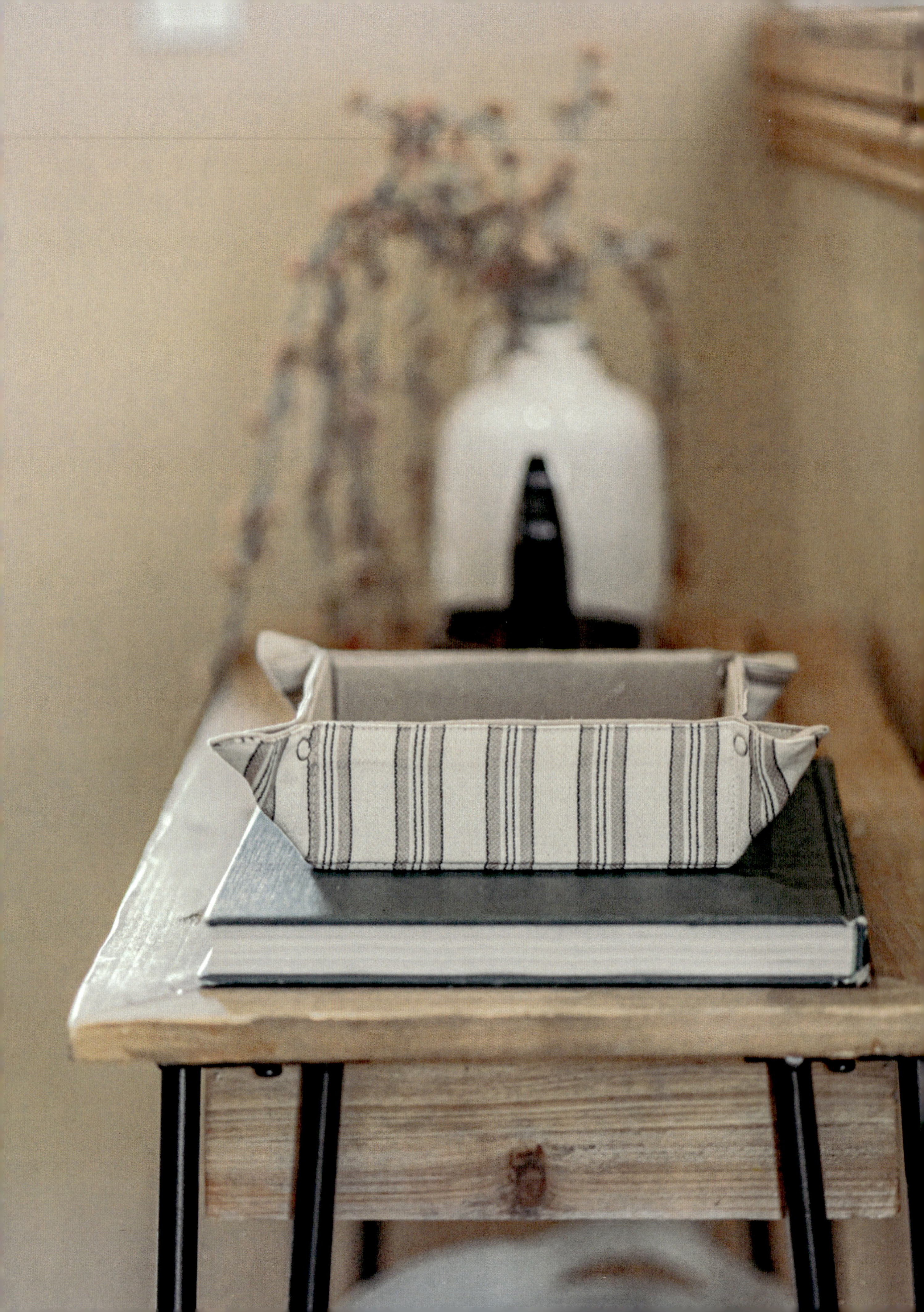

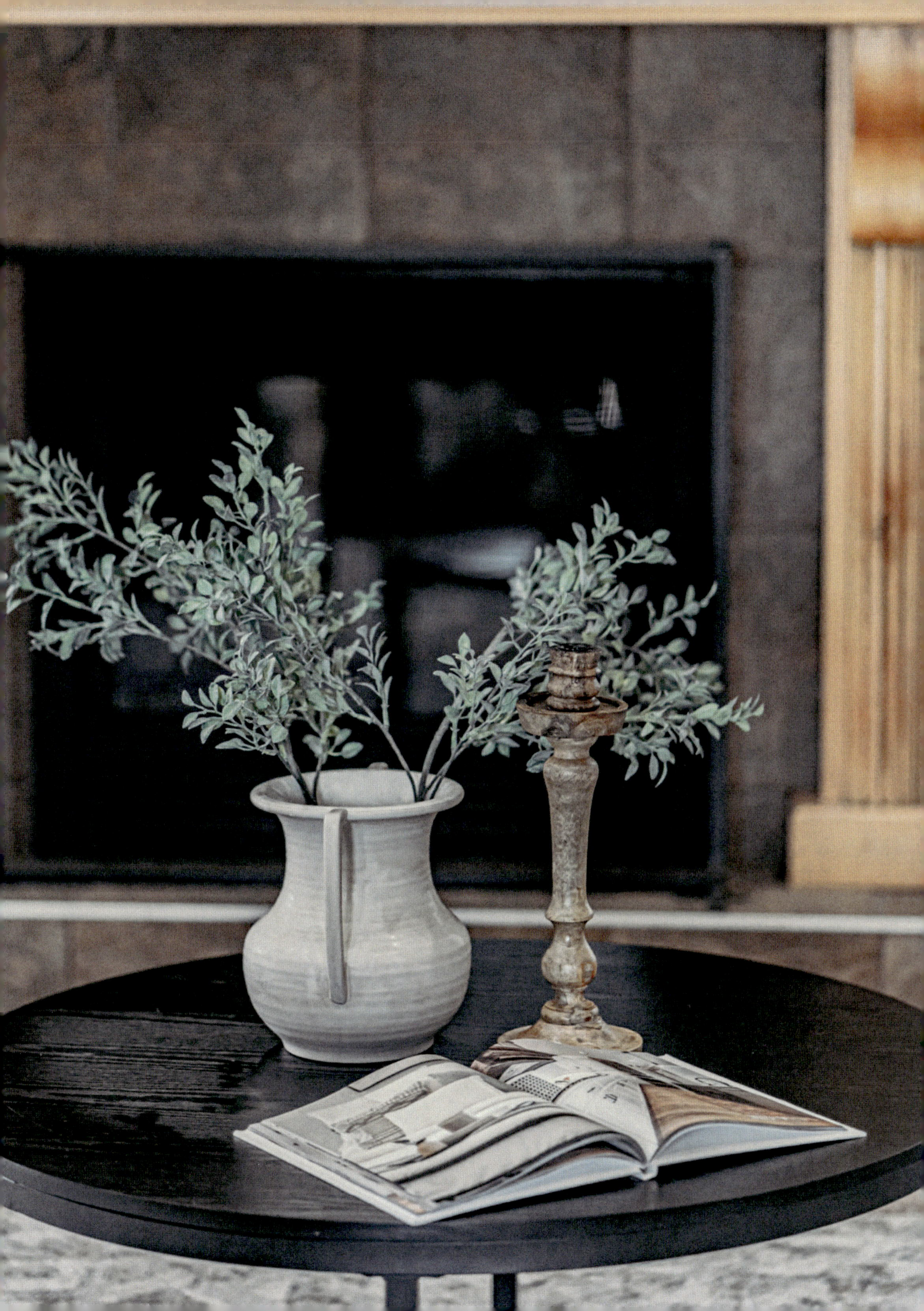

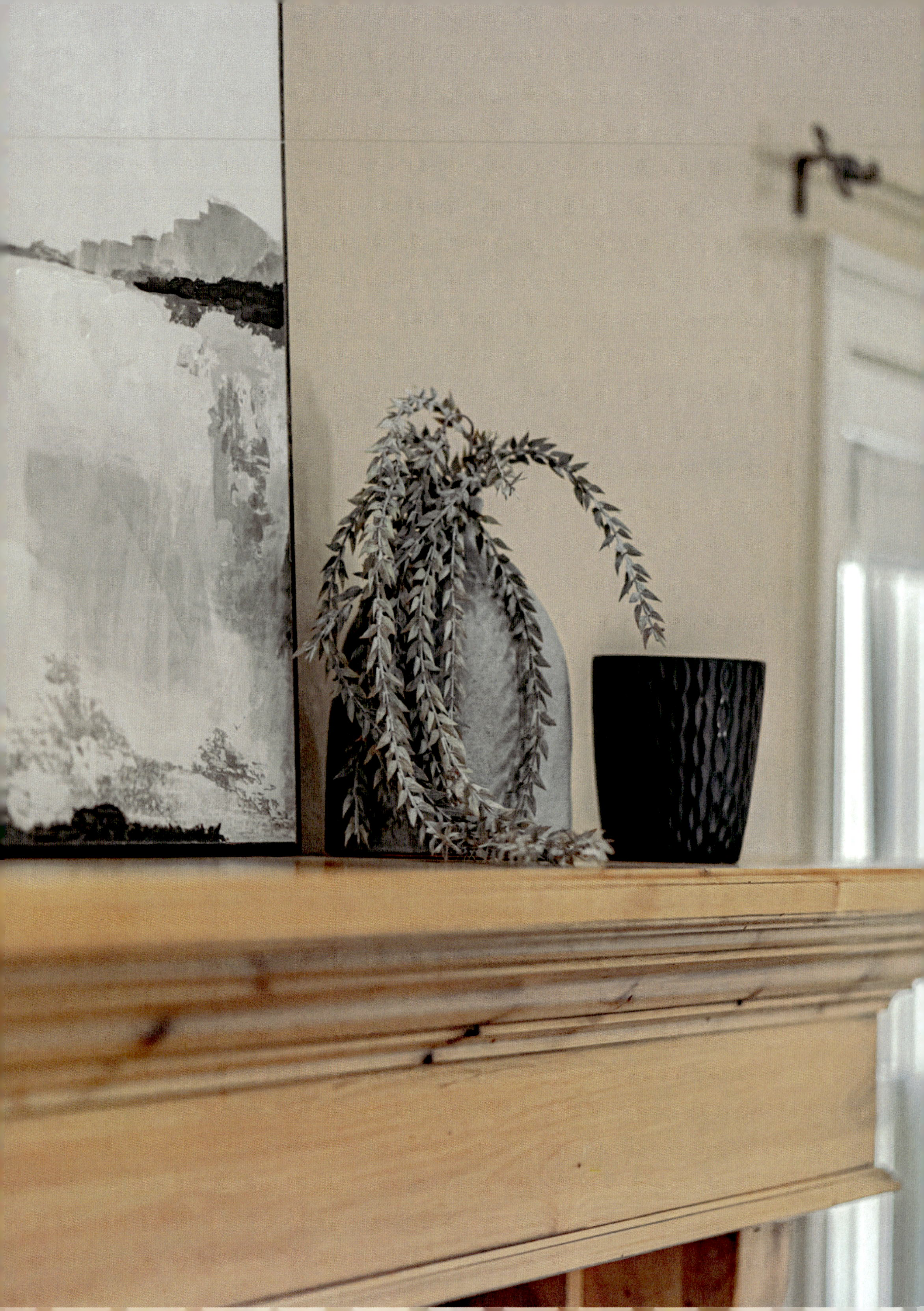

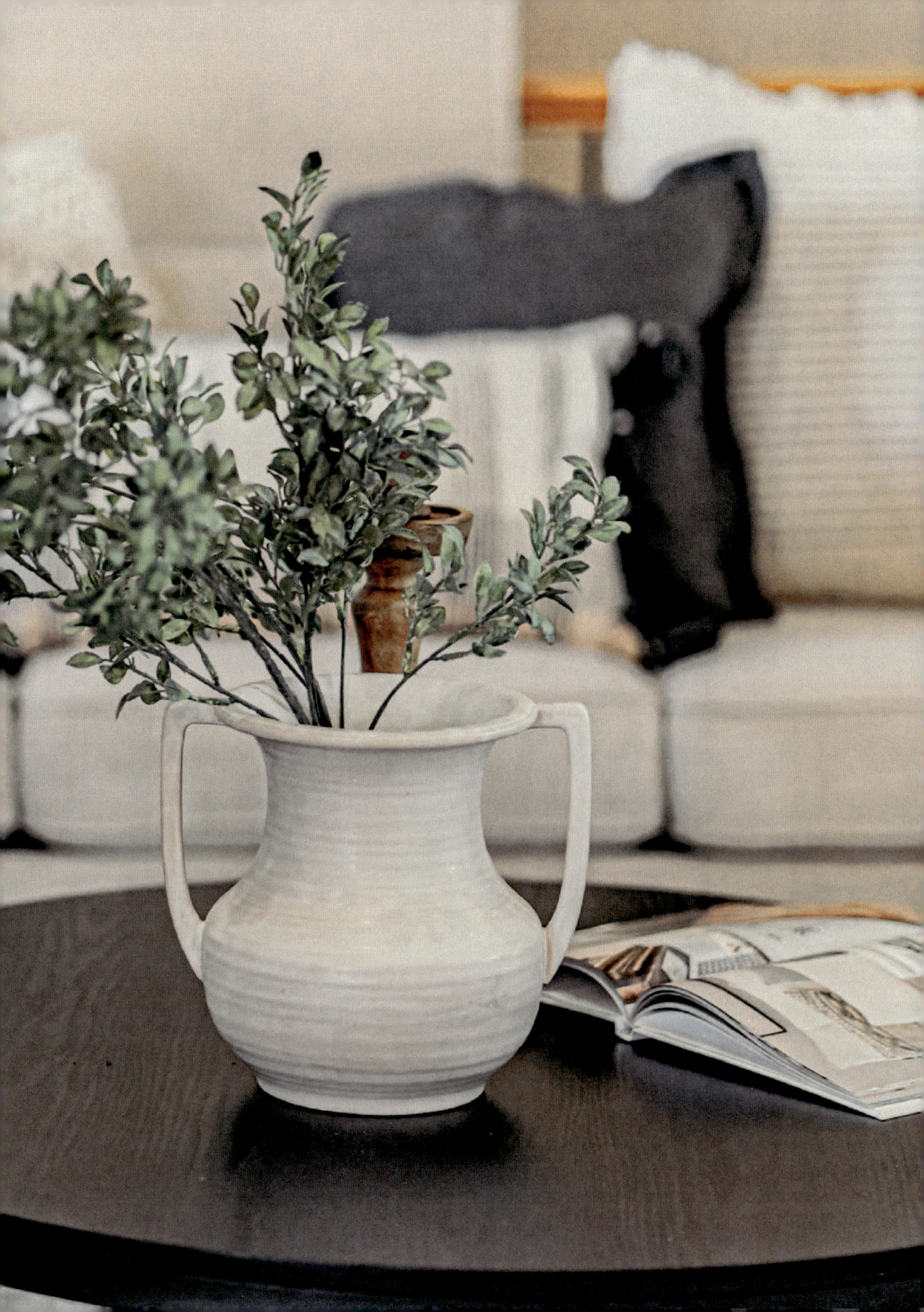

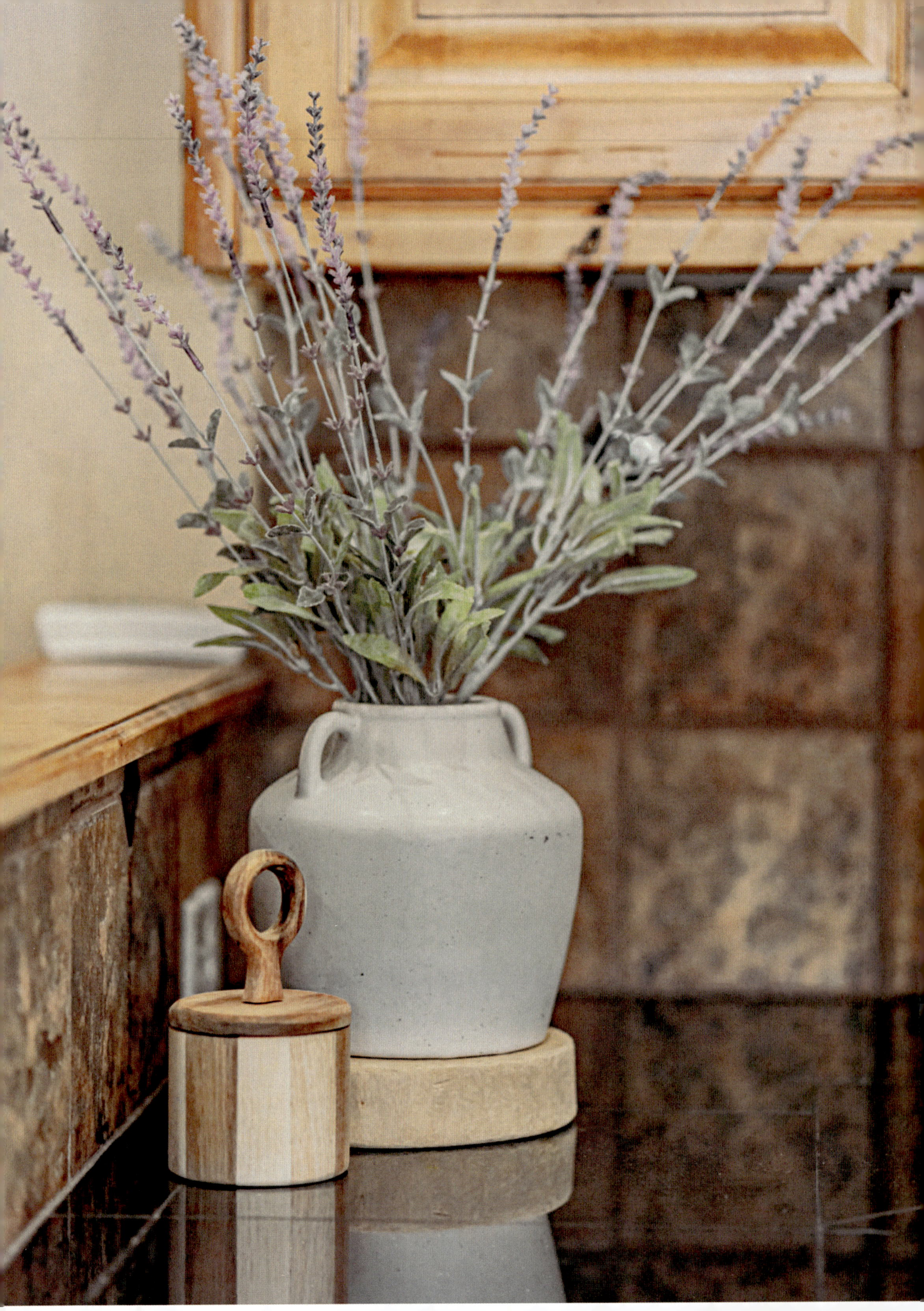

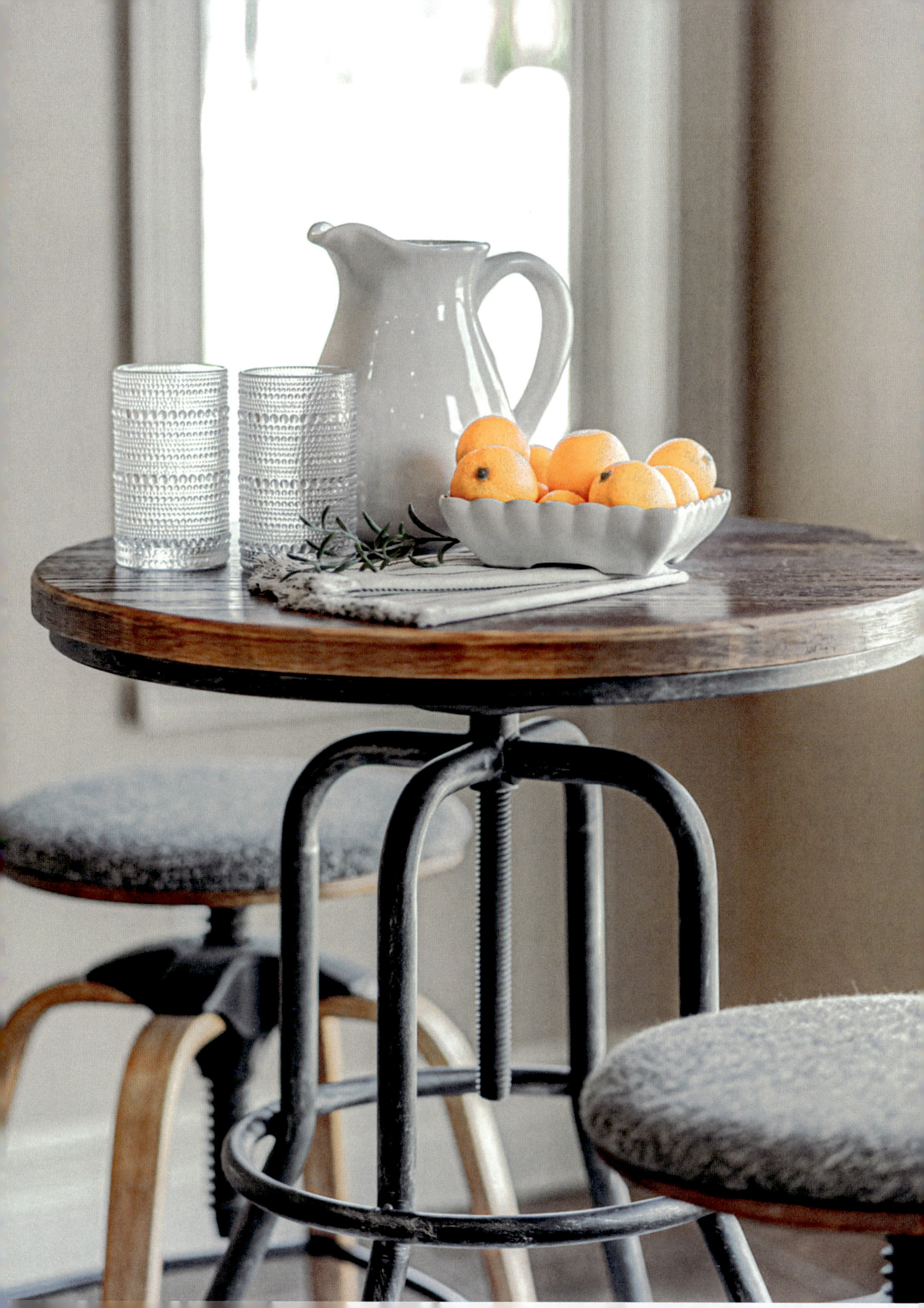

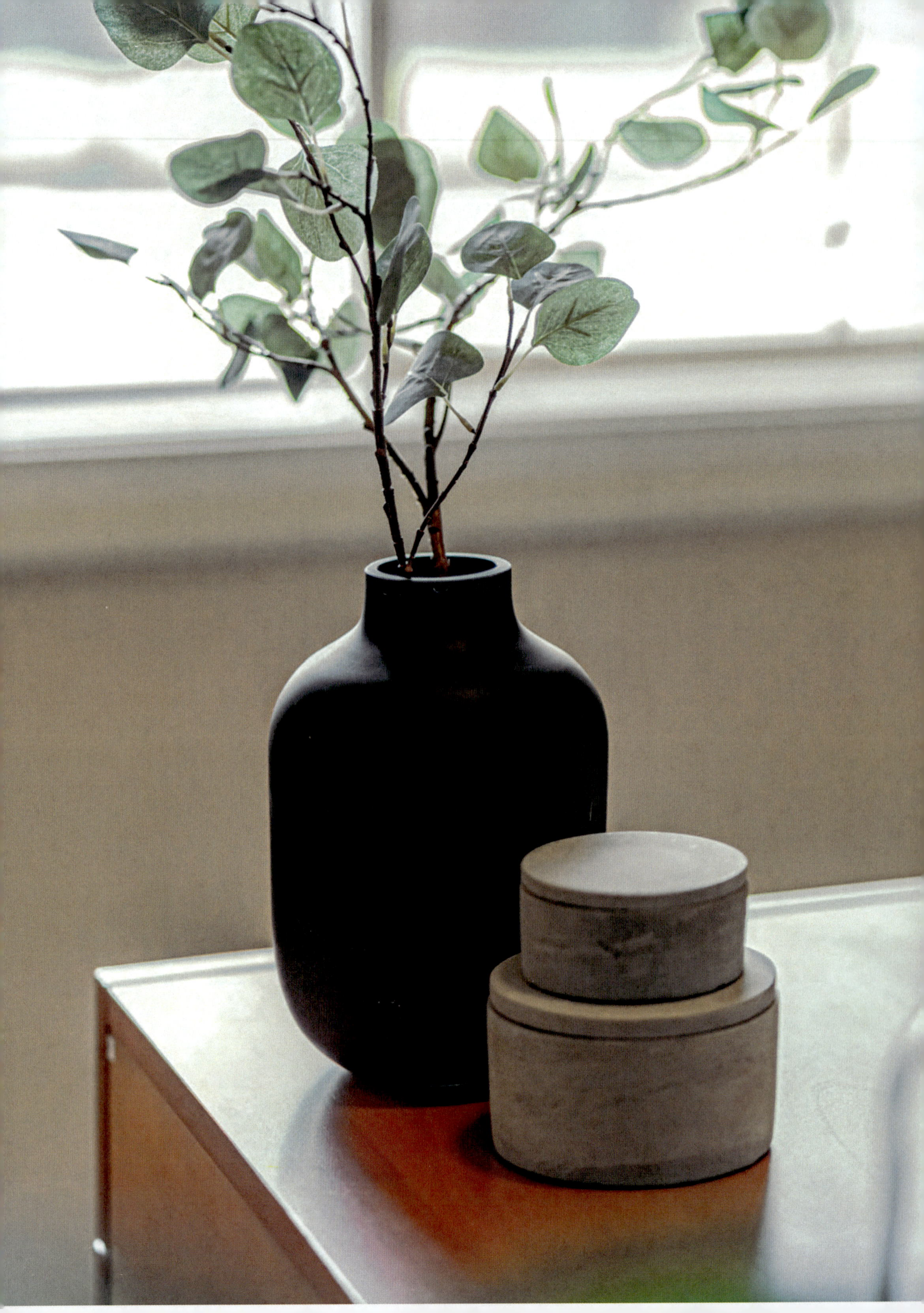

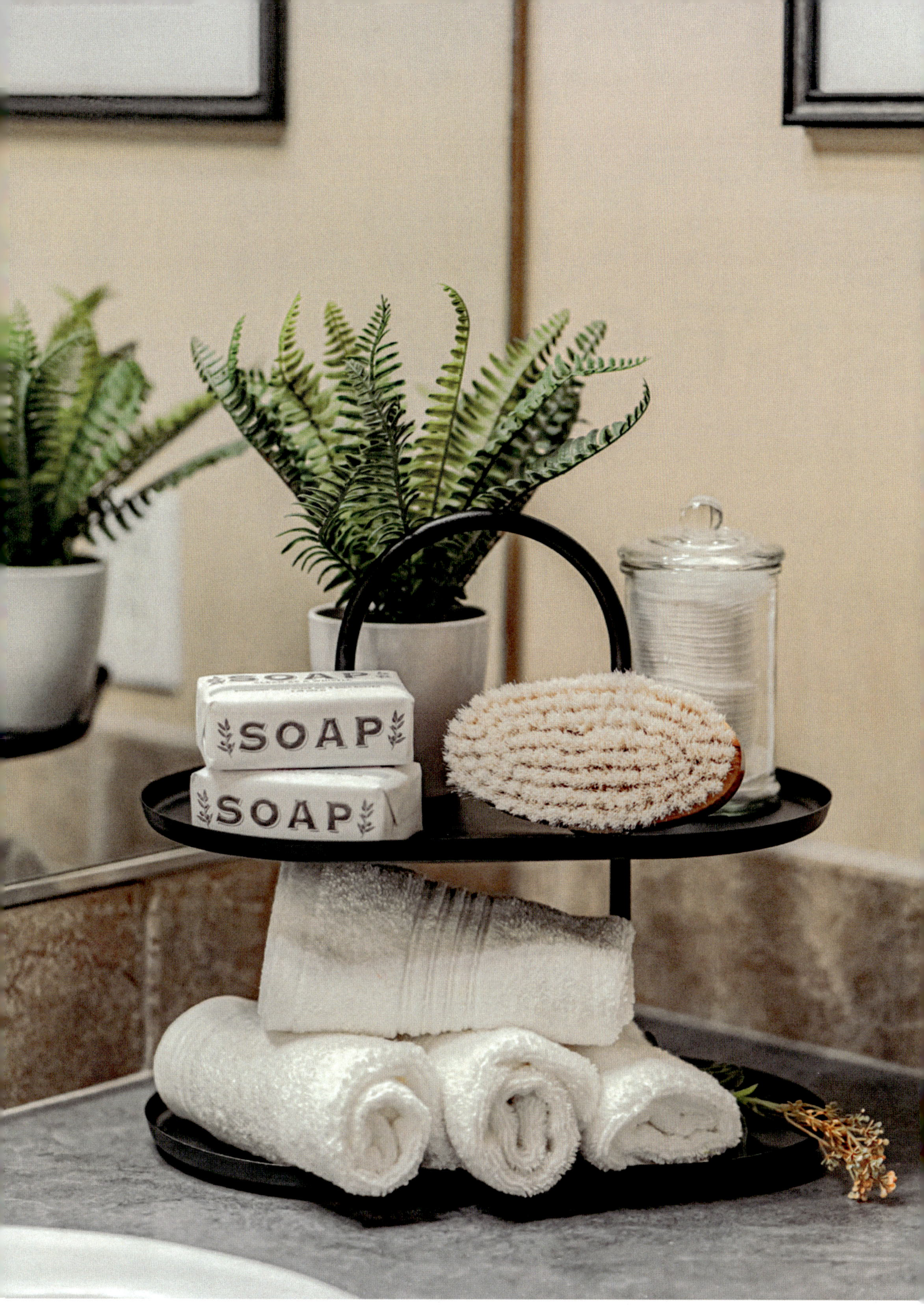
SOAP
SOAP

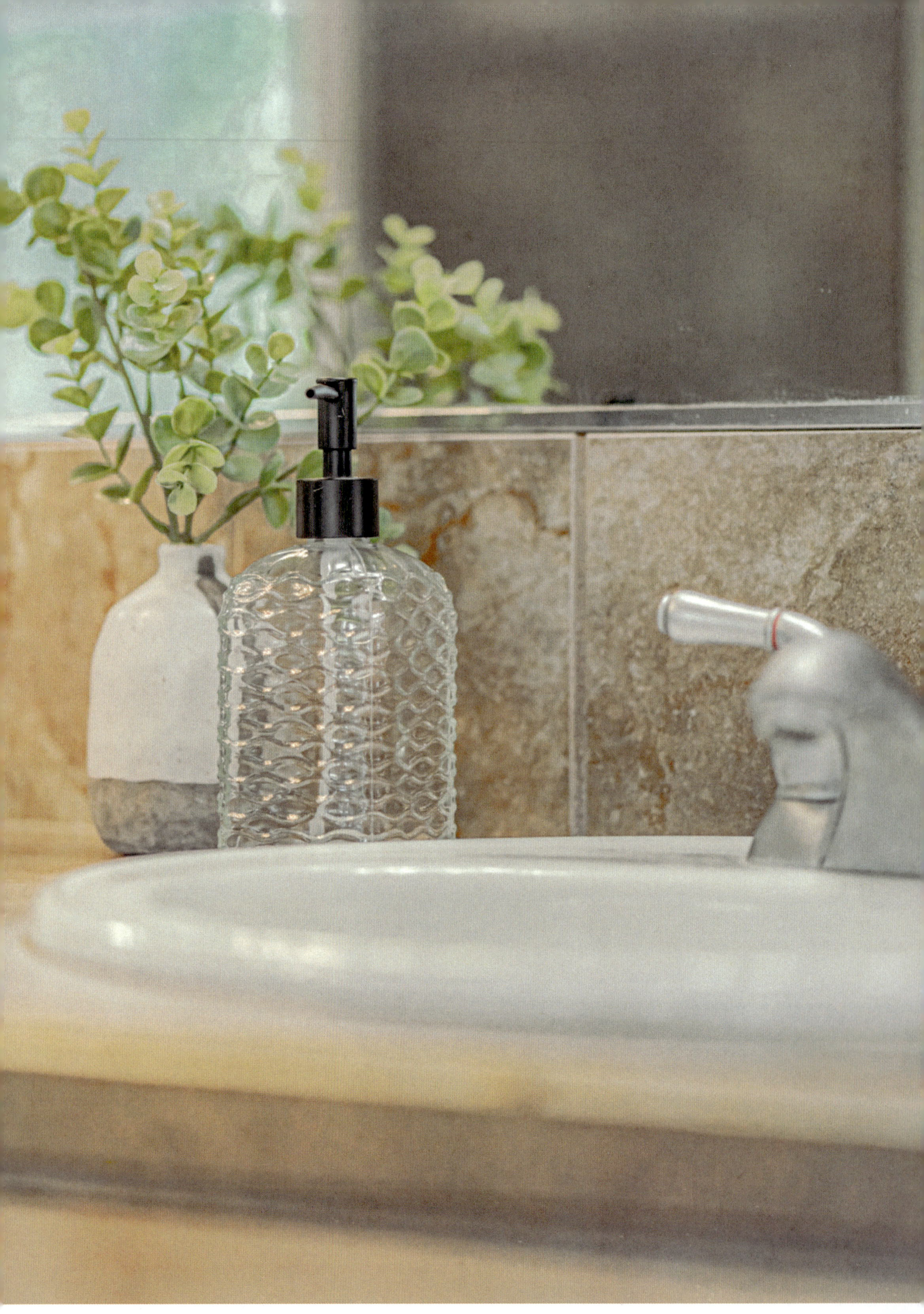

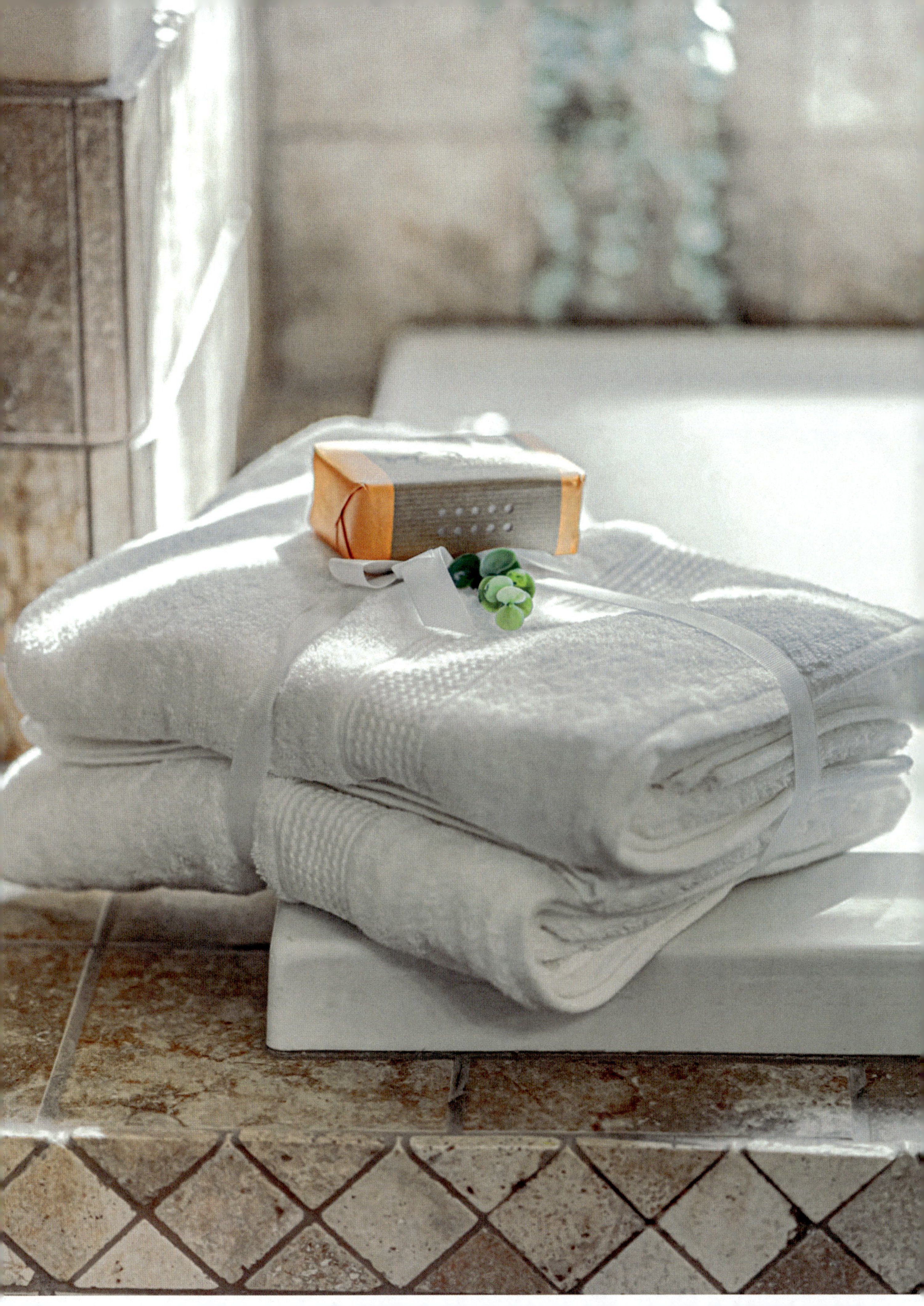

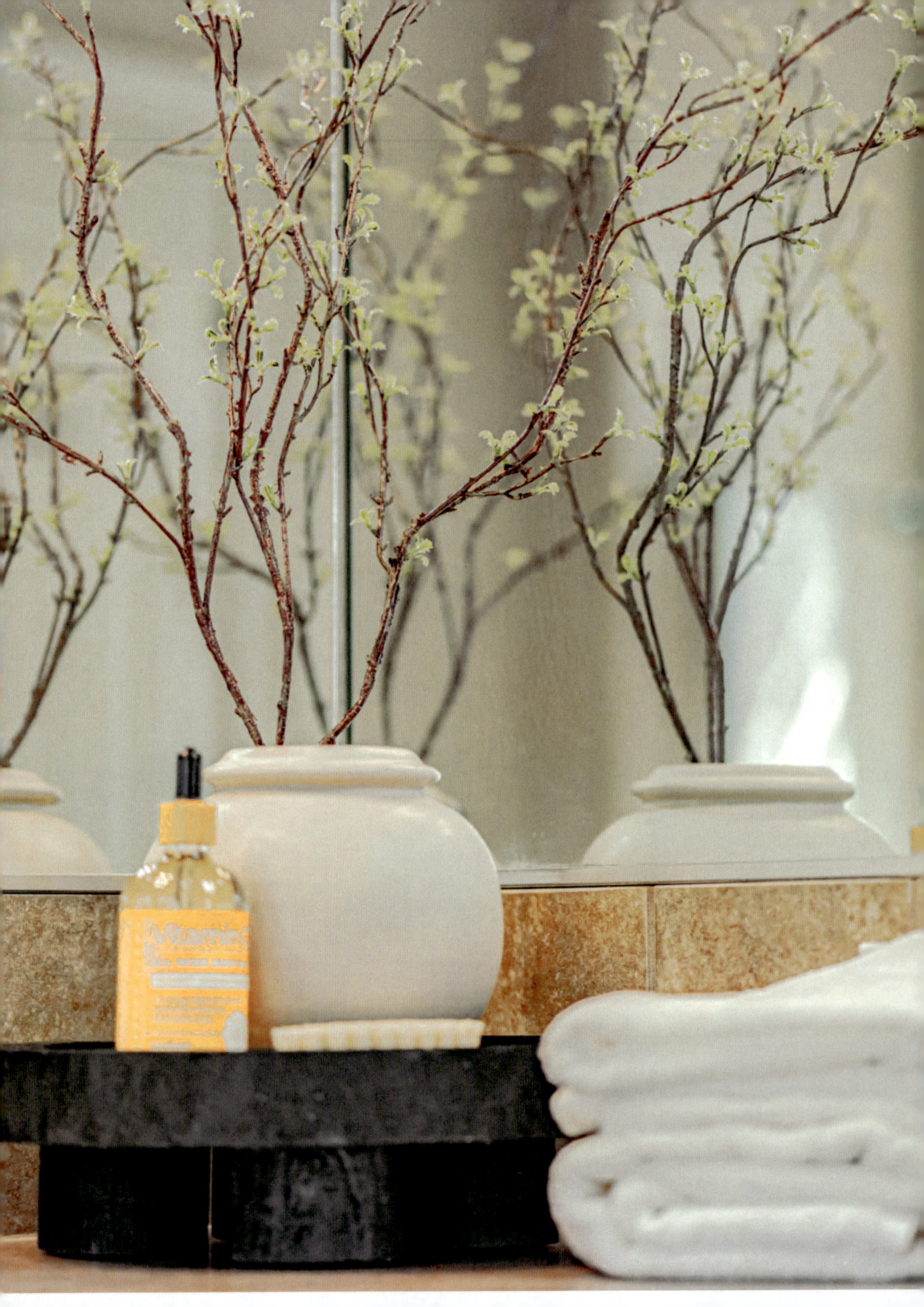

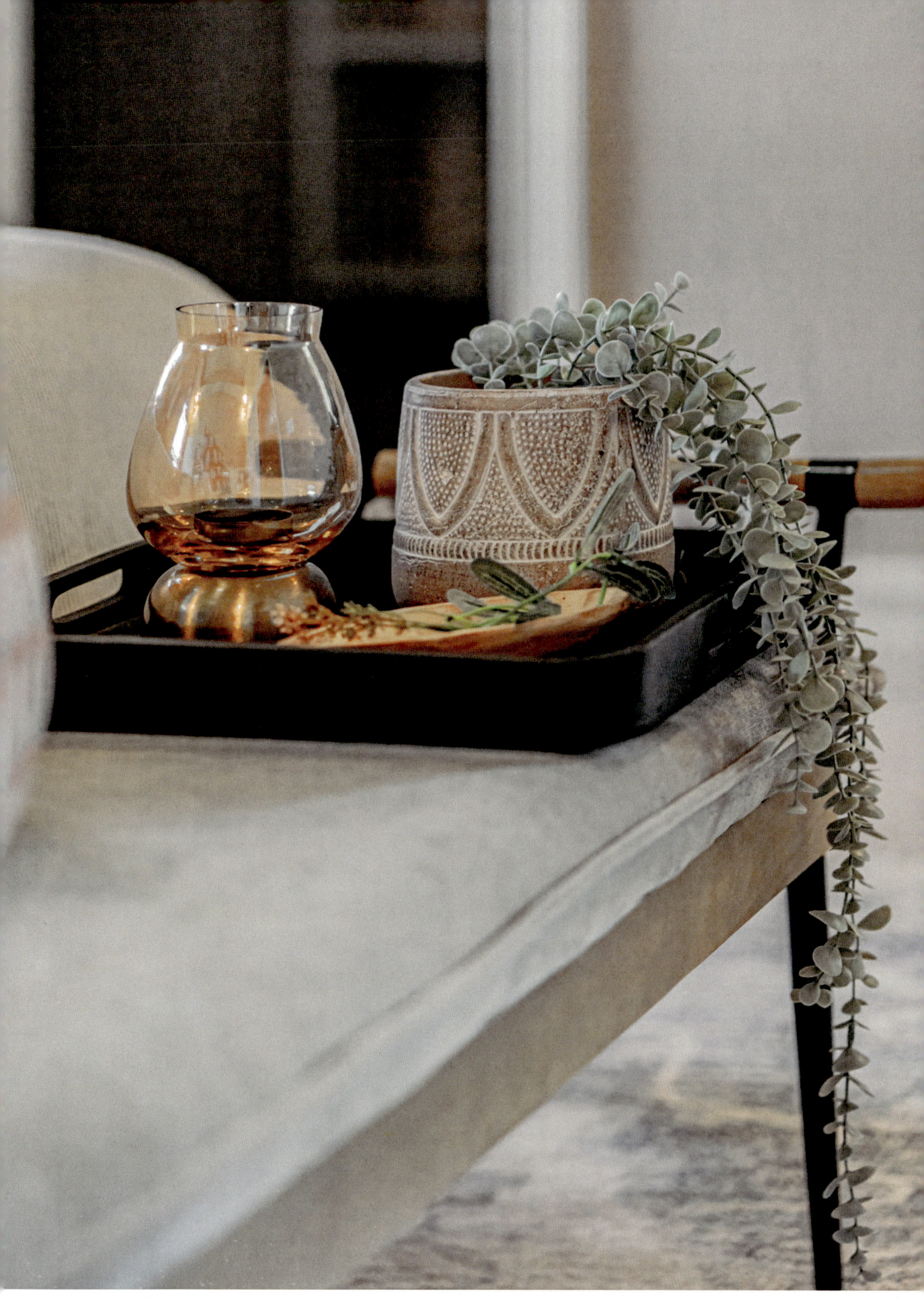

Made in the USA
Columbia, SC
19 March 2025

34375180-7e3c-4707-9b3f-d966a63b45ffR04